PUFFIN BOOKS

Editor: Kaye Webb

A Pony in the Lugga

How do you smuggle a pony into a hotel and on to a train without anyone finding out? Well, Nicholas and Anna managed it, even if their kind unsuspecting Aunt Tina had the most bewildering week of her life while it was happening.

It all began when Aunt Tina insisted on taking her nephew and niece on a trip to Copenhagen. She managed splendidly, even when Nicholas helped an old gentleman off the train with two suitcases belonging to someone else, and the children developed their eccentric passion for visiting the zoo. (For how could she guess that they intended to win a pony in a lottery?) Even at the hotel, when people in the room below began complaining of stamping and jumping noises on the ceiling, she still didn't guess, poor lady, that there really *was* a pony in the children's bedroom, or that they were planning to keep it hidden from her until they got it safely home. Surely disaster must overtake everyone. But does it?

This hilarious story by a prizewinning Swedish author keeps you laughing and wondering to the very end.

For boys and girls of eight and over, whether they love ponies or not.

Cover design by Richard Kennedy

Gunnel Linde

A Pony in the Luggage

Translated by Anne Parker
Illustrated by Richard Kennedy

Puffin Books

Puffin Books, Penguin Books Ltd,
Harmondsworth, Middlesex, England
Penguin Books Inc., 7110 Ambassador Road,
Baltimore, Maryland 21207, U.S.A.
Penguin Books Australia Ltd, Ringwood,
Victoria, Australia
Penguin Books (N.Z.) Ltd, 182–190 Wairau Road,
Auckland 10, New Zealand

First published in Sweden under the title *Med Lill-Klas i Kappsächen* 1965
Published in Great Britain by J. M. Dent & Sons Ltd 1968
Published in Puffin Books 1972
Reprinted 1973, 1974 (twice), 1975

Made and printed in Great Britain by
Cox & Wyman Ltd, London, Reading and Fakenham
Set in Intertype Baskerville

Contents

Illustrations

The Beginning of the Good Luck

It's amazing the luck some people have. For instance, they have an aunt who takes them for a trip abroad in the Easter holidays, all the way to Copenhagen, and lets them stand in the middle of the square in the capital of Denmark, and buy packets of sandwiches with double fillings – shrimps and bright yellow sausage and all sorts of delicious things that they have in Copenhagen. Some people are taken to Tivoli in Copenhagen and have rides on the switchback. But still you haven't heard the most important thing that happened. Really, it's unbelievable what luck some people have!

I am thinking of Nicholas and Anna. They were the ones who had Aunt Tina.

Aunt Tina was an exceptionally nice little aunt. She was so slim that your thumb and finger could meet round her wrist, and she always wore blue dresses: forget-me-not blue or dove blue or exercise-book blue, except on special occasions when she wore a peacock-blue dress with a gold pendant round her neck.

She lived alone in a prim little town somewhere far away, with a very old canary, and Nicholas and Anna had only met her five times when she came for a visit and said that she would like to take them with her.

To start with, Nicholas's and Anna's parents were absolutely against the idea. How could Aunt Tina possibly look after two of them, as she was not used to children? How would she be able to cope with all the difficulties and adventures that might crop up? And how could the children be sensible for a whole week and not cry with homesickness?

Nicholas and Anna promised with one breath that they would not feel the slightest little bit homesick, and Aunt Tina declared that the trip would give her much more pleasure if she could experience everything freshly through the eyes of children. Then came another bit of luck: Mother discovered that the decorators were coming to do the children's rooms the following week and of course it would be better if they were away.

So Nicholas and Anna packed and departed.

As soon as Aunt Tina had got them safely to the King Frederick Hotel on their arrival she sat down to write a reassuring letter to Mummy and Daddy in Stockholm. This is what she wrote:

My Dears,

The train journey went very well and we have arrived safely in Copenhagen. Anna lost her handkerchief as she waved good-bye and Nicholas helped an old gentleman off the train at Hallsberg and handed down two suitcases belonging to somebody else. Otherwise nothing has happened and we are all well. I knitted three tea-cosies on the way down. Tomorrow I will take the children to the Zoo for a while.

Kind regards to you both from Tina.

P.S. Don't worry. We shall not go in for any adventures.

That was what Aunt Tina thought.

'. . . we have arrived safely . . .'

Nicholas and Anna Try their Luck at the Zoo

The day they were going to the Zoo started very well. The sun was shining already when Anna pulled up the blind that morning. She and Nicholas had a room next door to Auntie's in the hotel. The first thing that happened was that the telephone rang on the bedside table next to Nicholas.

'Don't answer,' said Anna. 'It must be the wrong number. We don't know anyone in the whole of Denmark, so nobody could ring us up.'

'I could pretend to be someone else and have a bit of fun with them,' Nicholas suggested.

'No, don't do that,' said Anna. 'What if they get cross and complain to Auntie? We promised to be good, didn't we? Besides, it could be a kidnapper trying to find out if there are any children on their own in the hotel rooms.'

'Do you think so?' said Nicholas and lifted the receiver at once.

He was very keen to know what a kidnapper sounded like. But it was only Auntie. She wanted to tell them that she had slept well and was going to order breakfast in her room. They could do the same. She was looking forward to visiting the Zoo and seeing wild animals and perhaps having a snack and some tea at an outdoor café afterwards.

This Nicholas translated as 'fruit juice' to Anna. They had a race to see who would be ready first. Nicholas went out into the hotel corridor to look for his

. . . the keeper came and took the hat away . . .

shoes. He had put them out for polishing the night before – not by his own door but outside the one farthest away down the corridor, just to see what would happen. But the man who did the shoes was not fooled. He had put Nicholas's shoes back by the right door, so Nicholas only had to put them on. Soon the children were both ready and waited for Auntie outside the hotel.

There they stood looking nice. They were wearing their new travelling clothes. Anna wore her turquoise raincoat with a matching hat and her new shoes with stubby heels. Nicholas was wearing his red blazer with brass buttons. You could hardly notice the bulge of the hotel soap in his pocket which he had put in to give to the polar bears. They must need a lot of soap, he thought, to keep themselves so white. Anna looked at his newly cut hair and his serious expression and thought what a nice boy he was, considering he was a brother. Nicholas was the kind of boy who was always so busy enjoying life that he didn't even have time to smile. Of all the boys she knew, Nicholas was the one Anna would have chosen as a brother, excepting Tarzan, son of the apes, of course.

Nicholas was thinking that if there were no polar bears to give the soap to he could always pick up an old ice-cream paper and wrap it up to give to Anna. She would be sure to think it was strawberry ice-cream – it was such a nice pink soap. And she probably wouldn't tell Auntie either.

In a way, Nicholas rather liked Anna. If only she hadn't insisted on being two years older all the time he would have liked her whole-heartedly. It didn't even matter that she was a bit plump in places, in fact that was rather a good thing, as you didn't hurt yourself so much when you had to start a fight and give her a thump. He could almost say that as a sister she was OK.

The morning sun felt pleasantly warm on their clothes. They had to wait rather a long time, as Auntie thought that they were going to meet in her room and sat waiting for them there, but eventually they found each other and set out for the Zoo. They went by taxi.

'The Zoo is a bit like Skanksen in Stockholm,' Auntie told them. 'It is an animal park where you can see wild creatures from different parts of the world. I am sure you will find it interesting.'

She paid for them to go in and let them go first through the turnstile. As soon as they got in they saw how right she had been. In front of them they saw interesting sandy paths winding between various cages and in each cage was a different animal. First they came to an enclosure where beautiful frail antelopes and proud peacocks with trailing tails were walking about looking important.

'They must have got them all mixed up here,' said Nicholas.

Then he caught sight of a monkey mountain where a man had just dropped his hat down into the enclosure. At least twenty monkeys jumped down, trying to be first to grab the hat. They fought over it and tried it on and climbed up on the rocks with it and dropped it among the banana skins on the ground. Nicholas laughed and laughed, and when the keeper came and took the hat away he felt so sorry for the monkeys that he wanted to throw his cap down to them. But Auntie said 'No'.

'Oh look, there is an ostrich!' she called out as

... an irritated tiger walked backwards and forwards behind the bars ...

though that were the strangest thing she had ever seen. But it was just a bird that was much too big, jogging around on its own like a trapped long-distance runner. And that was just what it was, Auntie said.

Auntie behaved herself very well. She didn't try to hold their hands or tell them off in front of other

people. She just read the notices on all the cages out loud to herself, but that didn't matter very much. A bit farther on they came to a house for small animals. In there it was nice and warm and sort of sickly. There was a smell of guinea-pigs and musk-rats and mongoose.

'*Herpestes edwardsii*,' Auntie read out. 'This is an animal that kills poisonous snakes.'

'Oh, it's a Rikki-tikki-tavi!' shouted Anna. 'You know, like in the *Jungle Book*, Nicholas.'

Nicholas was disappointed. 'Is that what it's like?' he said as he looked at the quiet little animal with speckled fur creeping around on its own. Sometimes it lay down and rubbed its belly against the floor of the cage.

‘I think he ought to live in the snake-pit so he wouldn’t get so bored,’ said Nicholas.

‘Oh no, that would be awful for the snakes,’ Anna pointed out.

‘You’ve always got to feel sorry for somebody, haven’t you?’ Nicholas muttered gloomily. ‘Why shouldn’t I throw my cap down to the monkeys, anyway?’

‘Oh look, that is where they have the wild cats,’ Aunt Tina exclaimed.

It was a splendid building and Nicholas felt a great wave of excitement go through him as he opened the door. In there the smell was even more powerful. It was as if someone had waved rotting peppercorns around in the air. An enormous black panther jumped down from a ledge and stared at Nicholas and Auntie as if he had been waiting all his life for a chance to bite them. There was a loud thud as he jumped down, and he was much bigger than Nicholas had imagined.

In another cage an irritated tiger walked backwards and forwards behind the bars, breathing heavily through his mouth.

‘The poor animal,’ said Auntie. ‘Just imagine having an acute sense of smell for sniffing round a nice wild jungle, and landing up here in this stench. He is breathing through his mouth just to avoid the smell, I am sure. He ought to be let out!’

‘Poor us, then,’ said Anna.

‘People shouldn’t bring such a lot of animals here and condemn them to a life in captivity. I really can’t stand seeing animals in cages,’ Auntie said seriously as they left the building.

Then she caught sight of a black poodle sitting quite close to her, staring.

'Stand still, children! It's a baboon that has escaped,' she hissed. 'Shut him in at once!' she shouted to an unsuspecting keeper who happened to be walking past.

Nicholas and Anna felt very embarrassed that Auntie should be making a fuss over nothing. But the keeper just laughed and said that it was easy to make a mistake. He had often thought that baboons had faces like dogs, he said.

'Look, over there are the elephants, Auntie,' Anna said to distract her attention. 'Let's go that way.'

The elephants stood there lifting their feet as though they were dancing the Charleston in slow-motion. Nicholas held out his cap to one elephant, thinking that it would not be able to reach with its trunk. But the elephant could reach and politely took the cap and swept the floor with it before he threw it up on his back.

So that settled Nicholas's old cap, at last. Auntie gave him a good telling off but could not be bothered to be as angry as Mother would have been. In the elephant-house there were also a rhinoceros and some small hippos.

'Just look at that rhinoceros, his face is like a tortoise's if you take away the horn,' said Nicholas. 'Lots of animals are just like each other, really. If I didn't look carefully I would think that was a giant tortoise, wouldn't you, Auntie?'

'Nature cannot devise an endless number of new shapes,' Auntie replied patiently, pretending that she had forgotten about the cap.

Finally they came to a pleasant low house with a thatched roof that hung right down to the windows like a fringe.

'What a nice cage, do they keep human monkeys there?' Nicholas asked.

'Silly, that's one of the keepers' houses, of course,' Anna replied.

'First prize in the Great Zoo Lottery,' Auntie read on a notice.

Then she went over to a seat and sat down to get stones out of her shoes.

Just at that moment the adventure decided to present itself: Nicholas read on:

'You can win the whole house for just two crowns. You can have it put up on a site of your own choice, in-clu-ding furniture and the cost of the site. In-clu-ding furniture, what kind of furniture is that?'

'That means that you get the furniture as well,' Anna explained. 'What else does it say?'

'Second Prize: A tiger skin with stuffed head and teeth attached. Think of that! Third Prize: a polar bear skin. Fourth Prize: a live pony. Fifth to Tenth Prizes: Bicycles! Where do you get the tickets?'

Anna looked round. A small octagonal house with a pointed roof stood with its back to them on the other side of the gravel path some distance away. She thought she could hear the rustle of a drum turning with lottery tickets inside. Perhaps you bought the tickets on the other side of the house.

Auntie had not yet put her shoes back on.

'Let's walk round and have a look,' said Anna.

'Walk!' shouted Nicholas. 'Are you mad? Let's fly!'

Anna just about caught up with him as he vanished behind the little house.

'What do you want a house for? Surely you can't live on your own down here when the rest of us live in

Stockholm?' she pointed out as she caught up with him. 'Anyway, you can't look after a house, can you?'

'What makes you think I'm going to win a house?' he asked crossly. 'Don't you see, I'm going to win a pony!'

That was the good thing about Nicholas. You need never fear that he would do anything really silly. He pulled a bar of pink soap out of his pocket and found a Danish one crown piece underneath it. Without second thoughts Anna handed over her crown too. He took them both and thrust them on to the counter in front of the woman who was selling tickets.

'Could I have a lottery ticket, please,' he said. 'But it must be one with a prize!'

Nicholas and Anna continue as though Nothing had Happened

Auntie was still sitting on the seat suspecting nothing. Anna felt quite sorry for her. She almost wanted to go up to her and say: 'Never mind, Auntie. We can't help having such luck always.' But she didn't as it was better to let Auntie remain happy for as long as possible. Besides, they couldn't be *absolutely* certain of having won until after the draw. There are people who don't win anything in lotteries. The ticket was now in Nicholas's inside pocket carefully wrapped round the pink soap and could not get lost. The draw was in two days' time.

'Now let's go and have some tea,' Auntie said at once. 'I've been thinking of tea ever since you left me, and now I can't think of anything else. I can see a café over there, I think.'

Nicholas and Anna quickly took Auntie over to the tea-place and helped her to call the waitress. They saw that she got two teabags and two lumps of sugar before they settled down with their own sandwiches and cakes and glasses of raspberry-flavoured fruit juice that looked like the Red Sea.

After tea they spent as long again looking at things, just to be on the safe side. They saw owls and bears and Auntie caught sight of a whole lot of gentlemen in frock coats, waving their arms and paddling about in a pool of water. She thought they were business men having a look at the Zoo before they went out to dinner, and found it odd that they didn't change after the visit instead, until they got so close that she could see their beaks.

'Can't you see that they're penguins, Auntie?' Anna was very surprised.

Then Auntie laughed heartily and said that she couldn't see very far without her glasses. However, soon after that she began to get grumpy and tiresome and didn't seem to enjoy anything they did. She did not want to have a race to the reptile house or wait until the seal came up once more. The children understood that Auntie was beginning to get tired.

When she suddenly said: 'Now we must go home,' Anna and Nicholas both thought it was best not to contradict her.

'We have been here for almost four hours,' Auntie complained. 'If I had known it was going to turn into a trek through the desert, I would have brought my camel.'

Nicholas and Anna laughed dutifully.

'Some time or other one has to go home, and it's always best to go when you are enjoying yourself most,' Auntie said severely. 'That's why I think we ought to go at once.'

'Is a trek through the desert the thing you enjoy most then, Auntie?' Nicholas asked politely.

'If you are good now, and do as I tell you,' Auntie implored, 'we'll go and have a lovely dinner at Drachman's and you can choose your own dessert. Icecream with candyfloss, for instance. Surely that is better than horrible old baboons?'

'Can you really eat baboons with candyfloss?' said Nicholas in amazement.

But then it seemed just as though Auntie thought he was being cheeky. She stopped and looked from

Nicholas to Anna and then from Anna to Nicholas.

'Well, I'm going home, anyway,' she said desperately. 'And you two can do what you like!'

Nicholas and Anna were quite alarmed. Fortunately Anna thought of the right thing to say to get Auntie calm again.

'I'd like to go with you, Auntie,' she said. 'If you go, I'll go too.'

'So will I,' said Nicholas. 'I've managed to see the most important things.'

Then Auntie cheered up again. She got hold of a taxi that took them straight to their hotel. Anna and Nicholas shuddered at the thought of all the money Auntie was spending on taxis, but they said nothing. It was such a grand way of travelling, rather like being a film star or a millionaire.

Auntie sat between the children in the taxi. Nicholas leaned over and whispered to Anna: 'Shall we tell Auntie what we bought?' Anna glanced at Auntie who was staring out of the window without listening.

'Not yet. Let's keep it as a surprise,' she whispered back.

'Couldn't we tell her what we bought but not what we are going to win?' Nicholas suggested.

'Not a word,' Anna decided.

When they reached the hotel Anna took charge of Auntie.

'Now hadn't you better have a little rest?' she suggested. 'I'll come upstairs with you and cover you up with a rug.' Auntie looked quite grateful but unhappy at the same time. She probably didn't want Nicholas and Anna to be bored while she was resting.

'I'll look after Nicholas,' said Anna. 'He obeys me if I speak to him sharply.'

'And I'll look after Anna,' Nicholas added. 'She is so scared of me that I only have to look at her to make her tremble.'

'You must be nice to each other,' Auntie said, 'and don't go anywhere without telling me. I'm only going to have a little rest before dinner. Can I rely on you to look after yourselves in the meantime?'

'Oh yes,' they both answered. 'We won't go anywhere, just round the block to look in the shop windows.'

'You mustn't cross any streets. It is very easy to get run over.'

After that she allowed Anna to settle her down comfortably in her hotel room. Anna covered her with a pale blue blanket and a red rug and found her a book to read out of her big trunk. She turned the lamp round so that it would not shine in Auntie's eyes, and she drew the curtains. Auntie sighed contentedly and gave Anna two Danish crowns – one for herself and one for Nicholas, in case they needed money when they were looking after themselves. Then Anna went out and closed the door quietly.

Nicholas was waiting on the stairs. They looked at the time so that they would know when Auntie had finished her rest. Then they went out and wrote 'Buy lottery tickets' with the bar of soap at the nearest street corner. Nicholas felt that it was a pity that people didn't know what a good lottery they had at the Zoo. Good lotteries ought to be helped so that they would go on selling useful tickets instead of boring ones with dinner services as prizes. But when he got to the next street corner he realized what a mistake he had made. If more people bought tickets more people could win his pony instead of him. . . . Anna had to wait while he ran back and wrote something else. Now it read 'Don't Buy lottery tickets'.

'What shall we do with our two new crowns?' Anna asked.

'Buy another lottery ticket, of course, so that we can win a tiger skin rug as well,' Nicholas replied.

They walked round the block twice before they discovered a tobacconist's shop that must have been there all the time. They went in and bought another ticket for the Zoo lottery and wrapped that round the soap as well. Then they walked round the block once more.

It was really rather strange walking around on one's own abroad with all the people speaking Danish and all the pillar-boxes red instead of yellow as they were in Sweden.

'But I thought it would feel even stranger,' Nicholas said. 'I thought you would feel something in your feet when you trod on Danish soil.'

'What would that feel like, then?'

'Like the difference between gravel and sand of course, or between lawn and a stubbly field.'

'With your shoes on? Surely you can't feel that through your shoes?'

'That must be what's wrong then. Shall we take our shoes off and see if we feel anything?'

Anna did not want to, but in the end she went with Nicholas into a doorway and they took their shoes and socks off and walked around barefoot to feel Denmark. There was nothing special about it. When they got back to the hotel Aunt Tina had been awake for about five minutes. They went straight to Drachman's and had a very good meal with two desserts each.

While they were waiting for the bill Auntie wrote another postcard to Stockholm:

My Dears,

The visit to the Zoo was a great success. The weather was fine and the only event was that Nicholas dropped his cap into the elephants' enclosure. I will buy him a new one when we get home. The children got a little tired and difficult towards the end because of all the new impressions, but now we have had a rest and all is well again. I think Anna liked the antelopes best and Nicholas liked the mongoose.

Personally I have had enough of animals and I shan't set foot in the Zoo again in a hurry.

Kindest regards from Tina.

P.S. Not this side of Christmas, anyway!

That was what Aunt Tina thought on Tuesday.

Nicholas and Anna Hasten Slowly at the Museum

'Today we are going to the Glyptotek Museum,' Auntie said on Wednesday.

'Can you buy tickets for the Zoo lottery there?' Nicholas asked.

'Shhhh,' said Anna.

Auntie replied that they should have thought of that when they were at the Zoo, as the 'Glyptotek' was a museum where you could see beautiful sculptures by famous sculptors, but lottery tickets could not be bought there. And that was just as well, she added, as you never win anything in lotteries. Money down the drain, that's what it was.

Anna and Nicholas exchanged glances. It was awful to hear Auntie talking like that – what if she were right? What if they had spent Anna's two crowns and Nicholas's two crowns on nothing, when they could have bought ice-cream? Four crowns wasted, that would be dreadful. But Anna shook her head and raised her eyebrows at Nicholas as if to say 'Don't worry. That's just what Aunties say when they think one hasn't bought a lottery ticket and they want one to forget all about it to save the bother of walking for miles looking for somewhere to buy one.' Nicholas sighed and got ready to go to the museum.

Aunt Tina felt like walking. She kept cautiously to the very inside of the pavement close to the houses so that the children should not rush out into the traffic and get run over. But Nicholas and Anna stayed

There were lots of sculptures in the other rooms too

meekly beside her. First they went to the main square where they stopped to buy sandwiches. The sandwich shop looked like a hot-dog stand.

'How many sandwiches can you eat?' Auntie asked. 'There are several kinds to choose from: school packets, tourist packets, golden packets.'

'The golden packet sounds best,' Anna thought and Nicholas agreed with her.

'There are six sandwiches in those packets, can you really eat so many?'

'Of course we can,' Nicholas replied. So Aunt Tina bought a golden packet for each of the children and a school packet for herself.

After that they walked down a street called H. C. Andersen Boulevard and reached the Glyptotek Museum. It was a large, red-brick building with palms growing inside it. The palms grew right up to the ceiling and pink orchids grew out of the bark of the palm trees. There was a goldfish pond in the middle and a large marble lady lay there covered with little white marble children. The children crawled round her and up on to her from all directions. Anna counted and found that there were fourteen of them.

'This is a sculpture called "The Water Mother" by Kai Nielsen,' Auntie told them.

'Great,' Nicholas commented politely. 'Now we have seen that, we can go, can't we?'

Auntie explained that this was only the beginning. There were lots of sculptures in the other rooms too. Nicholas sighed. He stuck a finger into the goldfish pond to see if the fishes would get frightened but they did not. One came up and bit his finger instead. Auntie and Anna went on to look at the Egyptian sculptures.

'I think we ought to go to the Zoo instead,' said

Nicholas. 'You can see more lions and panthers there.'

'You'll find lots of animals here too,' Auntie coaxed. 'Just look at the monkeys and oxen and birds that the Egyptians painted on the walls of their tombs. Here a servant is holding a bird that wants to fly away. And there is a man carrying a deer. The Egyptians painted everything they thought the dead person needed on his long journey into the land of the dead.'

'I like real animals better,' Nicholas said. 'But not goldfish.'

'Just imagine, these pictures are from three thousand years before Christ!' Auntie exclaimed.

They continued into another room where marble heads stood on pillars all round the room.

'Is there a collection of skulls? Have head-hunters put out all their treasures here?' Nicholas suddenly appeared to be interested. But no. They were only portraits of Roman emperors which had been found in the ground. Nicholas became tired again.

'Give me baboons every time,' he said. 'I want to go to the Zoo again.'

Auntie pretended not to hear, and Anna decided that Nicholas was being a bore. She enjoyed looking at the sculptures. The heads looked like people she knew. One reminded her of the English teacher at school and another was just like an assistant in the butcher's shop at home in Stockholm. They were all different. What a lot of noses and eyes and chins! Anna decided she would only look at the noses so as not to get too muddled. If she looked at nothing else she might be able to remember all the noses in the whole museum until she got home and could draw them. It was difficult not to be distracted by other things, so Anna made field-glasses with her hands and peered through at each nose in turn. This made things easier, but by the time she had looked carefully at sixteen noses she had forgotten the first one. She lowered her hands to have a rest.

'Where did Nicholas go?' Auntie asked.

They both looked round. Nicholas had decided to disappear and was nowhere to be found.

'You go that way and look for him and I'll go this way,' Auntie said. 'Then we'll meet at the entrance.'

Anna set out. It was strange to walk through the quiet rooms all on her own. The only noises to be heard were people's embarrassed footsteps and her own shoes clattering along on the floor. She came into a hall where there were whole people made of marble, not just heads. Anna felt cold looking at them. There they stood so naked and still – she felt like wrapping them in blankets and looking after them. She came to a little sculptured girl lying flat on her face, crying. Anna stopped and patted her gently. Why was she crying? Anna tried to guess. Perhaps she had lost a little brother just like Anna, or maybe she had something even sadder to think about. Perhaps she had lost a Zoo lottery ticket and didn't have enough money to buy another one. Or had she thought that she might win a pony and then been disappointed? Anna's eyes filled with tears at this thought.

'Don't be unhappy, Anna, I have found him.' It was Aunt Tina.

'I'm not thinking about Nicholas, I'm thinking about this little girl who can't go to the Zoo,' Anna replied sadly.

'Now don't you start too!' Auntie snapped. 'Come and have your sandwiches with Nicholas. He is sitting by the goldfish pond with sandwiches lined up all round it.' Anna sighed and went off with Auntie.

The sandwiches were good. Anna had brawn on one, liver sausage on another, egg and anchovy paste on another, then ones with roast beef, scrambled egg and sardine, and bright orange sausage. She ate very slowly so that Nicholas should not be last and have something left over to tease her with after she had finished, but Nicholas was so slow that she simply couldn't wait for him. As she was swallowing the last crumb he still had a whole sandwich left.

'I'll keep that until I get to the Zoo,' he said, 'because I want to feed the ostrich.'

'I simply cannot understand why you want to go to the Zoo again when you have just been there,' Auntie complained. 'Surely it can't be much fun to go there again?'

'Oh yes!' Anna and Nicholas shouted at once. 'We *must* go there again. We can't live otherwise.'

'Oh well, I'll have to think about it,' Auntie said. 'But now let's go to Amalienborg and have a look at the changing of the guard.'

Anna and Nicholas were relieved. Perhaps if all went well they would have a chance of being at the Zoo when the lottery draw took place.

'Come along, Nicholas, don't keep Auntie waiting,' said Anna sternly.

After they had admired the soldiers with their great bearskins outside the Danish royal palace, Auntie brought out a postcard she had bought at the museum and wrote a few lines to Stockholm as usual:

My Dears,

Today we have done our best to improve our education, as you can see from the lovely sculpture on this card. We walked around the Glyptotek Museum for several hours. Nicholas was bitten by a goldfish, but otherwise he appreciated it all. The children can't forget what a nice time we had at the Zoo, and keep talking about going there again. But I shall think of something to make them forget all about it. Greetings from us all.

Best love, Tina.

That was what Auntie thought on Wednesday.

'Don't forget to tell them that we are going to the Zoo tomorrow,' Nicholas shouted when the band had stopped playing.

Nicholas and Anna and the Great Moment

'Oh, how lovely to be here again,' Anna said as they went in to the Zoo the following day. 'This is what I've been longing for all the time.'

'Me too,' said Nicholas. 'Look at those llamas. Aren't they lovely?'

'Yes, and the elephants,' Anna added. 'Aren't they funny the way they rock along.'

'I can't understand why you are so fond of animals,' Auntie said. 'I expect you'd like to take them home with you, but I won't have any of that! It's enough trouble looking after you two!'

Auntie laughed. Nicholas and Anna thought of a real live lottery prize that they would very much like to take home.

Now on the day of the draw they did not feel so sure of their luck any more.

'How many tickets do you think there are in a lottery like this, Auntie?' Nicholas asked, pointing at the first prize house 'including furniture' which they were just passing.

'Oh, a couple of thousand, I should think,' Auntie answered absent-mindedly.

'Thousand!' Nicholas shouted. 'Surely you mean a hundred? No, not a hundred, that is too many. American lotteries usually have ninety-nine, so there must be less than ninety-nine in this one because American things are always the biggest. Perhaps there are only fifty tickets, or, better still, only twenty-five.'

'Oh, no,' Auntie said. 'There must be more than that. After all, they have to be able to pay for all the prizes and still have money to spare, otherwise they would make no profit.'

'A whole house and lots of bicycles and rugs and live animals – that must cost millions,' Anna sighed. 'There must be no end of lottery tickets!'

'We'll say no more about it,' Nicholas snapped and looked at Auntie and Anna as though they had said something indecent.

He went on ahead to see if there were as many tigers as last time or if some of them had been made into rugs with teeth attached.

Anna took Auntie by the arm and led her to a comfortable seat under a tree and said: 'Shall we stop here?' Then she added:

'Wouldn't you like to sit down and take the stones out of your shoes? Nicholas and I can look around on our own so you don't get so tired, Auntie. We'll look after each other.'

'By all means,' Auntie replied. 'Of course I can sit down. I am afraid I can't oblige with stones in my shoes, but I have brought my knitting, so if I have to sit here I need not be idle.'

'Thank you, Auntie dear, we'll soon be back,' Anna said and rushed off to find Nicholas.

They had to find out if the distribution of prizes had taken place yet, or when it was going to be. They both hurried towards the little octagonal house where they had bought the tickets. The little house was shut and bolted, but there was a large notice on a shutter:

'Distribution of Prizes at 1 p.m. at the Bandstand.'

Nicholas and Anna started to run. The prize-giving

had already started! They had no idea where the bandstand was, but when they had rushed around aimlessly for a while they caught sight of a large crowd under the trees and guessed that that was the place. A man with a megaphone in his hand stood on a platform shouting to the crowd. Nicholas and Anna pulled up sharply so that they wouldn't crash headlong into all those people. They tried to push forwards into the crowd, but didn't get very far. They stopped to hear what was being called out. With trembling fingers Nicholas pulled the soap out of his pocket and unwound their tickets. One was number 96688 and the other one was 107. They heard the announcer shout:

'Ladies and gentlemen! The draw of the Copenhagen Zoo lottery has now been carried out and it is my great pleasure to announce the winning numbers. The complete list will be published tomorrow in *Berlingske Tidene* in the Personal Column.'

'I am so afraid that we have won that old house,' Anna whispered.

'We won't tell them, and then they can't make us have it. As long as we've won the pony on the other ticket!' Nicholas said.

Anna pinched him to make him quiet. The announcer had just looked at his papers and was raising the megaphone to his mouth.

'The completely furnished summer house to be erected on a selected site within ten miles of Copenhagen went to number 21303,' he shouted.

'Super!' Nicholas exclaimed.

'What luck that we escaped!' cried Anna.

They waited again. The announcer continued:

'The Second Prize, the newly prepared tiger rug

A man with a megaphone in his hand . . .

from the Zoo's superb tiger Maharaja who died of pneumonia last autumn, goes to 14211.'

Now that *did* disappoint Nicholas and Anna. It would have been fun to own a tiger rug, especially one with the whole head attached. Anna was planning to have it in front of her bed to lie on when nobody was looking. It would probably be very good to read exciting books on a tiger skin. Nicholas intended to have it under his desk so that he could put his feet on the head and pretend that it was a tame tiger waiting for him to finish his homework.

'Bad luck,' muttered Nicholas.

'What a shame,' Anna complained.

'The polar bear skin goes to number 14912,' the announcer called out.

'Not that one either,' Anna said. 'Our numbers are 96688 and 107. What sort of a rotten lottery is this?'

Nicholas stamped his foot.

'It's a dreadful cheat,' he said. 'They are just reading out pretend-numbers so that they can keep all their stuff. Those happy winners you see in the papers are only dummies that they have taken photos of.'

'Hush!' whispered Anna.

The announcer drew another breath:

'Now I should like to announce that the Zoo's great, great favourite, the miniature pony Daniel Pompiliam of Klampenborg, goes to 96688.'

'What?' said Nicholas.

'But that's our number!' said Anna.

Then they shouted out so loud that everybody turned round and stared. Anna grabbed Nicholas's arm and jumped up and down with him.

'It's crazy! It's impossible! It's not true!' she shouted. 'We have won him!'

Then Nicholas calmed down. 'Of course we have won him,' he said. 'Come on, let's go and tell Auntie.'

They rushed off in the direction of Auntie's seat – they both wanted to be first with the news. But the farther they ran, the slower they got. Finally Anna stopped altogether.

'Wait a moment,' she said. 'What if they don't let us have the pony?'

'Not let us have it? Why not?' Nicholas stared at her.

'Because it will make the flat untidy and that. And eat the curtains and refuse to go into the lift. Grown-ups are so fussy, you know.'

'Surely they can't take away our own lottery prizes?' Nicholas was appalled. 'Our own pony?'

'Oh yes, they can. "Cruelty to animals and ask-the-landlord," that's what they'll say. And Auntie's reply will be "Send-a-telegram-to-Mummy-and-Daddy-first". Surely you realize that?'

Nicholas did not answer. He dropped down on a seat and groaned. He could never have imagined such a crazy state of affairs. But Anna tried to comfort him.

'Of course we must have the pony,' she said. 'But we won't tell anyone about it just yet. Let's collect him first and take him home so that Mummy and Daddy can see how lovely he is, and then perhaps they will let us keep him.'

Nicholas cheered up.

'Yes, let's do that. It's not very far to Stockholm from Copenhagen. Just a straight run on the rails.'

'Bags I collect him,' Anna said quickly.

Nicholas looked miserable again, but this time it was only to make Anna let him have his own way. However, she saw through the trick.

'I am the biggest and most sensible,' she said firmly, 'so I'll collect him. Auntie is sitting over there. You go and tell her that I am lost and probably have gone straight back to the hotel. Don't say a word about our prize. But don't tell lies either – if you do they'll be cross with us afterwards.'

'Leave it to me,' Nicholas said. 'I can speak in riddles.'

He hung his head and walked with dragging steps towards Auntie. She was writing a postcard to Stockholm. This is what she wrote:

My Dears,

Here we are at the Zoo again and I am yawning just as much as the tiger on this card, but I hadn't the heart to disappoint the children as they were so keen on coming back. I think they imagined that they could buy tickets for the zoo lottery with some money I gave them, and perhaps win something nice to take back home. I told them people never win anything in lotteries, but they turned a deaf ear. Nicholas is just coming back now, and I can see even from this distance that he hasn't won a thing. But I shall cheer him up!

With best wishes from Tina.

That was what Aunt Tina thought on Thursday.

Daniel Pompiliam of Klampenborg

Anna hurried back to the announcer and wormed her way in between the people. She had to get right up to the platform to ask the announcer where to fetch the pony. At last she was standing by his feet and was able to pull his trouser leg. He was reading out a lot of boring numbers to do with bicycles.

'Here is the winning ticket, where is our pony?' she asked.

The announcer stared at her without understanding, then he turned round and pointed to the right.

Beside the bandstand stood a man in overalls holding a little brown and white pony, the smallest Anna had ever seen. And the shaggiest, and the liveliest, and the prettiest.

'So you are the young missie who has won our Danny,' the keeper said as she came up with the ticket.

'What a good thing that is; now he'll get a good home, I'm sure. Just what he wanted, a sturdy little girl who won't break in pieces if he kicks a bit. And someone with warm hands and blue eyes, he told me. So you're the right one, aren't you?'

What a talkative keeper! Anna would have liked to go off with Danny to some quiet place and just look at him. But the keeper wanted her to go along to the stables to fetch Danny's things. She patted the pony gently on the head and on the back. He shook his head and laughed.

... a little brown and white pony ...

'Dear Danny! My own Danny!' Anna whispered.

'He certainly likes you, missie, I can see that at once,' said the keeper.

'Is he difficult to look after?' Anna asked.

She was wondering how she would get him right through Copenhagen, as she didn't even know the way.

'Oh, no, he's as peaceful as a lamb, but as stubborn as a red pig too of course. All miniature ponies are. They are full of defiance like small children all their lives, because they never grow any bigger, do they? You've looked after horses before, haven't you, missie?'

'Well, no,' said Anna timidly. 'I mean . . . that is . . . in a way of course. Nearly, that is. I've had a canary.'

'Well, well, well, that's almost the same thing, isn't it? You just have to feed them with bird-seed and see that they don't fly away, and it's the same thing with ponies, only they have to have carrots and grass and bran and they must be groomed and shod and exercised so they don't get too fat. Otherwise it's the same.'

'Yes, I'll remember that,' Anna promised.

'I'm sure you'll manage,' the keeper said. 'Don't forget to scratch his forehead and pat his right flank if he is difficult. He likes that and it will calm him down, you see. Now, if you would just sign this receipt, missie, the pony's yours.'

He handed her a ball-point pen. It was a strange feeling to sign a paper of horse ownership. Anna felt butterflies right down inside her.

Carefully and slowly she wrote 'Anna Nilson' on the dotted line. Then she returned the pen and took Danny by the mane.

'Come along then, let's go,' she said.

But it was not as simple as that. The Zoo would only send its charges out into the world in a fit and proper state, so the keeper had to put a halter on Danny, and Anna was given a blanket, a scraper and a brush for grooming in a shoulder bag, and a little sack of hay and carrots to carry. The keeper gave her a pocketful of lump sugar to fall back on until Danny had learned to obey her. At last she was allowed to go. She led Danny round the corner from the stables and then she stopped to have a look at him all by herself, as she had planned. He looked back at her and shook his head again. He really was the prettiest pony ever!

'If they don't let you go to Stockholm, Danny, I shan't go either,' she told him as they walked along.

They went past the monkey house and the snakepit. Danny sniffed at the snake-pit and put his ears back as they passed the monkey house. By the bird pond he stopped and wanted to drink. Anna could see nobody around who would mind, so she let him drink. The flamingoes looked reproachful, but Danny neighed and frightened them away. She patted him for being so good. Anna intended to pass quite near the place where Auntie had been sitting to see if Nicholas had managed to get her off home, but just as she was looking out for Auntie's blue coat she was suddenly surrounded by a lot of men with cameras in their hands.

'Here she is!' they shouted. 'Stand still a moment so that we can take a picture for the papers!'

Anna obligingly put on her photo face, but then she remembered that she didn't like having her picture taken, and besides, she did not want to get into the papers either. What if Auntie saw the picture! But the men already had their cameras poised and were turning them this way and that, coming closer and closer.

'There now, smile, please! One, two, three, snap!' one of them said and his camera went click.

Anna just had time to put her hands in front of her face.

'No, no, no, that won't be any good,' said the photographer and started again. 'You mustn't be shy, dear. You've won a lovely pony and everything. . . . Now we'll try again.'

'Click!' Anna screwed up her eyes and pulled a face.

'Now, no nonsense!' shouted another photographer and shook his fist. 'Of course you want your picture in the paper.'

'I can't help it. I always do this when people take pictures of me,' Anna mumbled.

By now the photographers were all impatient and they clicked their cameras so quickly that Anna found it quite difficult to keep up. She pulled faces, frowned and stuck her lips out so that she would not be recognizable. Everybody got rather cross. The only one to laugh was Danny. He lifted his head and neighed which made them all jump. Then he set off at a gallop right out of the crowd. Anna only had to follow him. They ran all the way to the peacocks' enclosure.

'Well done, Danny!' Anna panted when she caught up with him. 'Now we must help each other to find the hotel.'

She looked round in all directions to make sure that Auntie was nowhere to be seen. Lots of people looked at her and many children wanted to pat Danny, but Auntie and Nicholas did not appear.

Anna took a firm grip on Danny's halter with one hand and his sack of hay with the other and walked straight up to the exit of the Zoo. She had a good look to make sure which was the right-hand side of the street, and then she set out for town, leading Danny on that side.

Nicholas and a Four-legged Worry

Nicholas was sitting in the hotel room with Aunt Tina, holding her hand. Nicholas hated holding people's hands, but he felt he had to make a sacrifice just for once. He felt so sorry for Aunt Tina. She was terribly worried. First Nicholas had rushed round the Zoo with her, trying to find Anna, and he had been afraid all the time that he really might find her by mistake. Then Auntie had asked a keeper to make an announcement about Anna over the loudspeaker to tell her to get in touch with the hotel as soon as she could. Then Nicholas and Auntie had rushed home in a taxi to get back before Anna telephoned. Nicholas was quite worn out. But that was nothing compared with what Auntie was.

'I must telephone the police,' said Auntie. 'I must call the Rescue Brigade. I must ring the Zoo. Oh, why did I drag out two innocent children into the wide world and abandon them among tigers and polar bears . . . How could I?'

Nicholas tried to comfort her. 'But you haven't lost me yet, Auntie,' he said. 'It's only Anna who's lost.'

'*Only* Anna,' wailed Auntie. 'How can you be so heartless about your little sister, who is roaming around among lions and tigers?'

'She's not little,' said Nicholas. 'She's twelve years old, and anyway, she can't be roaming about among the lions. She'd never get though all those bars and things.'

'But what if she doesn't find her way back to the hotel? She may have misunderstood what they said over that dreadful loudspeaker. Perhaps she's looking for us all over Copenhagen. I must telephone the police. I must ring the Zoo. I must call the Rescue Brigade.'

Nicholas let go of Auntie's hand and started walking up and down the room. He tried to glance out of the window without Auntie noticing it. He wondered how far Anna had got.

'Can't you wait a little longer, Auntie? I'm sure she'll be here any moment. She got very good marks in Geography, and she did Denmark ages ago at school. I'm sure she will find her way.'

Auntie looked at Nicholas as though he had given her a glimmer of hope. But then hope faded and she was just as worried as before. 'What will Mummy and Daddy say?' she asked. 'Whatever will they say?'

'Yes, I rather wondered about that too,' said Nicholas. They looked at each other.

Suddenly they heard the sound of someone running outside in the corridor. Nicholas dared not turn round. But Auntie gave a scream of joy. She recognized the sound of Anna's footsteps. The door was flung open and sure enough, there she was.

'Nicholas, come out a moment,' she said. Auntie stretched out her arms.

'Anna,' she cried. 'Anna, where have you been? Darling child, we have been so worried.'

'Oh dear, have you been worried? I won't be a moment, but there's something I've simply got to do.'

But then Auntie got angry. 'Out again! Are you quite mad? Now! When we've only just found you!'

'Yes, I really must. I only want to tell Nicholas

something.' She ran up to Nicholas and whispered, 'He's terrific. Brown with white spots just like a cow and I left him downstairs in the reception place.' She was just about to rush off again.

But Auntie planted herself firmly in the way. 'Oh no, you don't, miss. There's something I'd like to tell you. People simply don't run off leaving their aunt at the Zoo, letting her die of fright and then just refusing to talk to her. What do you mean by standing there whispering about pigs and cows? As if I didn't know everything about animals too, after being dragged to the Zoo day after day! I know what it's all about.'

Anna stared at Auntie, and then glanced inquiringly towards Nicholas. Had he told her anything? Nicholas understood what she was trying to say. 'No, no, of course not,' he said. Anna heaved a sigh of relief. She went up to Auntie and flung her arms round her.

'Poor Auntie, have you been worried? But I was all right. I came straight here as fast as I could. Of course I had to ask hundreds of people before I could find the way. And they all speak Danish so it's awfully hard to understand what they are saying.'

Auntie gave Anna a hug. 'Did you come all the way by yourself, you poor little thing?' she sighed.

Anna nodded. Auntie thought it was in reply to her question, but it was really a signal to Nicholas who was standing by the door, waiting to run downstairs and take charge of the pony.

'Come along, Auntie, let's go out on the balcony. I'll show you exactly how I got here,' was the last Nicholas heard as he closed the door behind him and rushed down the corridor. When he got to the entrance hall he stopped. There was nobody about, not even at the reception desk, where a tall porter usually sat staring at everyone who walked past. It was just the right moment for leading away a small pony. But where was it?

Nicholas turned round on the red carpet and saw himself in all the mirrors. Whatever had Anna done with the pony? Just then there was a sort of snuffling noise from the other side of the reception desk. Nicholas stretched across the desk and looked down. There he was, the world's sweetest pony, and his tail was so long that it touched the floor. Nicholas climbed over the desk and gave Danny a welcoming pat. And Danny nudged his hand and nodded. He was really no bigger than a St Bernard dog. Now, the question was how to get him upstairs.

Nicholas took him by the mane and made encouraging noises. Danny allowed himself to be led as far as the stairs, but there he stopped and looked doubtful. 'Come on, surely you can walk up ordinary stairs,' said Nicholas.

Danny hesitated and looked as though he wondered if he really could. But then he sighed and started plodding up the stairs. When they reached the top, they came to a corridor with rows of doors on either side. How could they get past without meeting anybody? Nicholas clenched his fist. 'Typical,' he muttered. 'They tell you all about horses as vertebrate animals and what kind of teeth they have and so on and so forth. Biology books are just full of the stuff. But not a word about useful things like how to get a pony upstairs into a hotel bedroom.'

One of the doors in the corridor was open and Nicholas could hear a chambermaid humming to herself as she worked. He crept towards the door, hoping that he would be able to close it. And then he caught sight of a pile of blankets. He cautiously stretched out his hand and pulled a blanket towards him. It might come in handy. Suddenly he heard footsteps at the other end of the corridor. There was only one thing he could do. He unfolded the blanket and draped it over Danny so that not even his head was showing.

It was the porter. He stopped in front of Nicholas with a stern expression on his face.

'Where are you off to?' he said. Nicholas tried to sound nonchalant.

'I'm going to Room 119. We live there.'

'And what's this then?' The porter pointed at the bundle of blanket that was Danny.

Nicholas swallowed. 'This? Oh, this – well you see, it's Danny, my brother,' he said. 'We're playing horses. Gee up, Dan. Come along.'

The porter looked at the disobedient bundle of blanket. 'He doesn't seem to be very well trained yet. He won't do what you tell him,' he said, laughing. 'Off you go, up to your room; you mustn't carry on like this in the corridors. The hotel blankets aren't here for you to play with, you know.'

Nicholas wanted to go at once, but Danny wouldn't budge. He just stood there under the blanket. 'Come on, Danny, off we go.' Nicholas felt desperate. All would be well if Danny kept quiet, but of course he didn't. He let out a funny neighing sound.

'Would you believe it,' said the porter. 'Quite a good imitation. Not bad at all. He ought to go on the stage, your brother.' The porter was just about to pat Danny through the blanket, but fortunately at that moment Danny decided to move off, followed anxiously by Nicholas.

'Well I'm blessed, the things children get up to. You might almost think it was a real horse.'

Nicholas led Danny past Auntie's door and into his own room. He turned the key twice in the lock.

'Quiet now, Danny, while I make you a stable in the cupboard,' he said.

Anna Stays Away from the Round Tower

'If we put some hay and carrots in a shoe box for him he will probably manage if we have to go out,' Anna said the next morning when she had opened the door of the wardrobe, which was really a built-in cupboard, and said good morning to Danny.

They had taken all their clothes out of the wardrobe so that Danny should not get scared in the dark, and they had given him the plastic waste-paper basket to drink out of during the night. Danny seemed lively and happy as he gazed at them from under his fringe.

'Who is going to clean up for him?' Nicholas asked as he peeped into the cupboard. It looked as any stable would when a horse has spent the night there: straw scattered about and horse-droppings on the floor.

'We must try to borrow a dustpan and brush and throw all that down the lavatory,' Anna said earnestly. 'You stay here and talk to Danny.'

She went out into the corridor and looked round for a brush.

The cleaners had started their work and were bustling about in the rooms, but of course they were using the brushes themselves.

'Excuse me, may I borrow the dustpan and brush if you can spare them?' Anna asked.

'You don't have to sweep up, dear. I'll clean your room later on,' the cleaner said kindly.

'But I'd like to do it myself – I *love* sweeping,' Anna said.

Danny seemed lively and happy as he gazed at them from under his fringe

'Here you are, then,' the cleaner replied. 'But bring them back soon. I have a lot to do.'

Anna hurried back to their room. She swept the wardrobe clean, emptied the waste-paper basket and placed it upside-down over the dustpan so that nobody could see what she had swept up. The cleaner was still there when Anna came past again and Anna dared not look at her as she slipped into the lavatory. She flushed the dustpan and wiped it with several paper towels before she gave it back.

'I have tidied up so thoroughly that there is no need for anyone to come and do our room,' Anna told the cleaner. She did not look particularly grateful and it was hard to tell whether she would come in or not, but Anna hoped for the best. She hurried back to Nicholas.

'Open the cupboard door and all the windows,' she whispered. 'We don't want a horsey smell in here.'

Nicholas flung open the windows and let the sunshine in. Anna led Danny up to the window-sill for a little fresh air. He snorted with pleasure. Then he put his muzzle on the window-ledge and sniffed in the traffic fumes.

'Look, Danny, there's the dairy we came past yesterday,' Anna whispered in his right ear and pointed to the shop.

'And in that direction is the station we are going to travel from tomorrow,' Nicholas whispered in his left ear.

Danny nodded as though he had understood.

Anna happened to glance across the road, and she caught sight of a woman in a window opposite standing there looking odd.

'Look out, someone is staring at Danny!' she whispered.

'Look, Danny, there's the dairy . . .'

Nicholas pulled Danny's head in and stared back angrily.

'I'll glare at her until she thinks that she has seen a dog,' he informed Anna.

But Anna was getting worried.

'I don't think we dare leave him, somebody might come in if we are not here,' she murmured. 'I had better stay at home with him.'

She backed Danny into the cupboard again and scratched his head. There was a knock at the door. Anna just had time to give Danny another carrot and shut him in before Nicholas opened the door a few inches. It was Auntie.

'Can't I come in?'

'Oh yes, of course, do come in, Auntie. I just wanted to see who it was first, one has to be so careful, you know.'

Auntie was all dressed to go out with coat and gloves.

'I thought I'd take you to the Round Tower today,' she said. 'It's a most interesting tower which was built three hundred years ago. There is a telescope for looking at stars on the roof and you can see the whole of Copenhagen too.'

'I have heard that one can see the stars from any place, as long as one sits somewhere dark,' Anna told them. 'If you sit in the bottom of a well, for instance, so that the light doesn't reach you, you can see stars in broad daylight.'

'I have never heard that before,' Auntie said politely, 'but perhaps it's true.'

'Yes, I'd much rather stay at home to see if I can look at the stars from the hotel,' Anna went on. 'I can draw the curtains so it gets quite dark, and I'll sit over here in the corner peering out.'

'That is quite the silliest idea I have ever heard,' Auntie declared. 'You can't see any stars from here. And what is the fun of sitting in the pitch-dark, anyway? No, of course you must come with us!'

'But I feel so tired,' Anna moaned. 'My legs feel as though they were going to break in half and I can hardly stand up.'

She sat down hastily on the bed.

Auntie gave her a searching look.

'Of course, you walked too far yesterday,' she said finally. 'Why don't you tell us the truth, then, that you are tired? I don't want to drag you off to the Round Tower if you don't feel like it. You get back into bed and have a good rest. Nicholas and I can look at the Round Tower on our own.'

'Come on, then, Auntie, let's go at once,' Nicholas said impatiently. 'Don't let's stand here getting mouldy.'

There was a thumping noise in the wardrobe. Danny was changing feet and must have thumped his hoof against something.

'What on earth is that noise?'

'It must be one of the maids bumping around with the vacuum cleaner,' Anna explained hastily. 'She has been out there all the morning making that noise.'

'I am sorry we shall not have you with us,' Auntie said. 'I was planning to take you to the King's Garden for lunch. It is quite close and would be very convenient.'

'I can have lunch here in my room,' Anna suggested. 'Couldn't you ask them to send it up to save me going out? I don't mind at all if you and Nicholas have lunch at that place.'

'You're a very good girl, Anna,' Auntie said. 'Well, let's do that then. Look after yourself, dear.'

Nicholas opened the door so that they would get out quickly and Auntie waved to Anna.

They stopped at the porter's desk and ordered lunch for Anna at twelve o'clock.

'I must ask the children not to stamp and jump so much in their room,' the porter said. 'We have had complaints from the floor below. It is better if they play horses out of doors.'

Auntie stared at him in amazement.

'The children don't bang about,' she said. 'It is the cleaner with her carpet sweeper in the corridor. I heard it myself just now.'

'Well, then I must apologize,' the porter said. 'I have to comply with the wishes of our guests. But of course they could be mistaken.'

Nicholas said nothing. He just longed to get away, and he felt sorry for Anna who would have to struggle alone with all the hotel cleaners and porters until after lunch.

Auntie brought out her map of Copenhagen and found the Round Tower. It was not far. They only had to walk past the Church of Our Lady and down Great Kannikestreet. Nicholas soon spotted the tower above the rooftops. They found the entrance and Auntie paid for both of them to go in.

From below the tower did not look very high, but it took a long time to get up.

'Why are there no stairs in here – it is just one long steep hill,' Nicholas said.

'Yes, that is strange,' Auntie agreed.

She got out a booklet about the Round Tower which the keeper had given her and began to read.

'One could get right to the top in a racing car and

down again on roller skates,' Nicholas remarked as he struggled uphill.

'Here we are!' Auntie had found the place in the book. 'Tsar Peter the Great rode all the way up this tower when he came to look at the stars through the telescope, and his wife followed him in a carriage drawn by six horses. I suppose they found it more convenient to drive up, as lifts had not been invented.'

'Was the whole tower built for horses?' Nicholas exclaimed. 'I wish I had known!'

'What would you have done then?' Auntie wondered.

'I would have brought a horse I know,' Nicholas replied.

Auntie laughed. Nicholas was about to tell her that it was nothing to laugh at, and that he meant it, but he stopped himself just in time.

They struggled slowly up towards the top of the tower. Half-way up there was a little room with a telescope and many strange things from the times of Tycho Brahe, the astronomer. Nicholas looked at everything and then they continued up to the top of the tower.

Up there Nicholas put a coin in the telescope and turned it round to look at the view of Copenhagen. He tried to find the window of Anna's hotel bedroom to see what she was doing with Danny, but it was no good. On the way down Nicholas ran as fast as he could down the indoor hill. He kept to the outside wall to get the full curve and to get a good speed up. Auntie kept to the inside where the hill turned on itself. In this way she had a much shorter distance to walk and could take it gently while Nicholas ran for all he was worth. She still got to the bottom at the same time as he did.

'I got to the barrier first!' Nicholas shouted as Auntie stopped to buy postcards by the exit.

'Wait a little, we must send a card to Mummy and Daddy,' said Auntie and wrote:

My Dears,

Nicholas and I have just been up the Round Tower. Imagine me struggling up a spiral hill more than 100 feet high! I had to think about the pattern of my latest tea-cosy to avoid getting giddy. Nicholas would have liked to ride up, but unfortunately he had no horse. What an idea! – where would he have got one from? Now we must hurry home to Anna who is having a quiet rest in the hotel to get her strength up for tonight when we are going to Tivoli.

Greetings from all of us, Tina.

That was what Auntie thought on Friday. She posted the card and called gaily to Nicholas.

'Now we will go to the King's Garden to have a look at a statue of the great writer Hans Christian Andersen. You remember his story about the tinderbox don't you? With a dog who has eyes as large as the Round Tower?'

'Is the statue outside or indoors?' Nicholas asked.

'Out of doors of course. The King's Garden is a park, you see.'

'Is there grass round the statue?'

'I should think so. Are you so hungry that you intend to eat grass?'

'It's not for me,' Nicholas replied. 'But I'll take some back for Anna. There's nothing she likes better than fresh grass. It's true, you know!'

Tivoli or Not?

'I thought you would never get back,' Anna said as the door closed behind Auntie and Nicholas sat down with a sigh on the edge of the bed. 'I've had such a to-do! First the cleaner came and wanted to tidy up. I had to say that brooms give me hay-fever to make her go. Then a man from the floor below came up and said that he would report me to the management if I didn't stop jumping up and down in here. After that a waiter brought my lunch and at that moment Danny decided to neigh.'

'What did you say?'

'I said it was the man in the room below, laughing. But that's a lie. I don't think he has ever laughed in his life,' Anna said crossly.

'You poor thing,' said Nicholas. 'And we are not leaving until tomorrow, worse luck. What if Auntie drags us out tonight as well? Then something dreadful will happen!'

'We simply mustn't leave Danny alone for a single moment,' Anna declared.

Auntie had gone to her room to change for dinner. As it was their last day, and everything was to be particularly festive, she was putting on her peacock-blue dress with the gold pendant. She had told Nicholas to brush his hair, and Anna was to wear her best dress.

'We have to go down into the dining-room for a little while, but we must take turns to come up and have a look at him. I have wound my hat round one of his front feet and your flannel round the other one. My flannel is round one of his hind feet – but I didn't know what to put round the fourth one. It was silly of you to give your cap to the elephant.'

'Well, what did you use?'

'I took your pyjama jacket, and that's not much good either, because the buttons rattle. But it will have to do.'

Anna lay down on her stomach on the floor and rooted round among the clothes under the bed to find her best dress. They had had to hide all the clothes there, otherwise Auntie would have wondered why they were not hanging in the wardrobe. The dress looked rather crumpled.

'Hurry up, so she doesn't come back again,' Anna whispered. 'We'll give him his food just before we go so that he can occupy himself eating while we are away.'

Nicholas scratched through his hair with the comb and Anna flung her best dress on as quickly as she could. Auntie came out of her door as they stepped into the corridor.

'I must just buy a paper and find out the times of the evening amusements,' she said with a mysterious air as they went downstairs.

Nicholas and Anna shuddered.

They trooped into the dining-room together.

'We want the very best you have to offer,' Auntie said gaily to the waiter as she opened the paper.

'Chicken, and afterwards ice-cream with hot chocolate sauce?' the waiter suggested.

'Yes, please,' Auntie decided.

'I like sausages and fried potatoes better,' Nicholas said. 'But I'll eat whatever you give me. At least if it is ice-cream with chocolate sauce.'

She was staring at a picture on the back page of Auntie's paper

Anna said nothing. She was staring at a picture on the back page of Auntie's paper. It was rather blurred, but she could see quite clearly that it was a picture of herself with Danny beside her. 'The happy winner of the Zoo's miniature pony was Miss Anna Nielsen' it said. What if Auntie turned the paper over?

Auntie glanced at the front page for a moment before she opened the paper out.

'I wonder if the amusement guide is at the front or at the back?' she said.

'Probably at the front – almost certain . . .' Anna said.

'No, it doesn't seem to be,' Auntie replied.

She turned over a few more pages. Anna stretched up so that she could see how far Auntie had got. Only a few more pages now. Just two or three, and now she had reached the last page but one. She sat there staring at the paper.

'What is it?' Nicholas asked.

'I can't find what I am looking for,' Auntie replied. 'That is very odd!'

Anna stared at Nicholas intently, to stop him from looking at the paper. She was not sure that he would be able to keep their secret if he suddenly caught sight of the picture. Nicholas just stared back crossly without understanding what it was all about.

Anna glanced at Auntie. Then she noticed that Auntie was looking at them in a troubled way over the top of the paper.

'I think we'll eat first and think about the next step afterwards, otherwise we'll get no peace.'

'I think so too,' Anna agreed.

'But the food hasn't come yet. Let me look at the cartoons in the meantime.'

'Nicholas!' Anna burst out. 'One doesn't read at the table!'

'Auntie is doing it, so why shouldn't I?' Nicholas retorted crossly. He couldn't understand why Anna didn't want him to look at the paper.

'Let him do as he likes, as it is the last day,' Auntie said reasonably.

She sat back in her chair and stared straight ahead. Nicholas opened the paper.

It could not be helped. As Nicholas was holding the paper, the picture on the back page was exactly on a level with Auntie's eyes. Her gaze seemed to rest on the picture of Anna and would have burned a hole in the paper just where Anna's face was, if her looks had been burning rays. But it was difficult to say whether Auntie really saw what she was looking at or if she was just staring without seeing.

Anna clasped her hands tightly under the table and thought: 'If I keep my hands together all the time she will notice nothing.' She clenched her fingers so hard that it hurt. Suddenly Auntie focused her eyes and frowned. Her eyes moved as though she were reading. Anna could have sworn that Auntie had been reading the text under the picture of the pony. But she kept her hands clasped all the same. Auntie said:

'Now put the paper away immediately, Nicholas!'

Nicholas looked up in surprise.

'But I've only looked at the first strip,' he said.

'That's enough,' Auntie declared. 'There's nothing but bad news in the papers.'

She took the paper and folded it first one way and then the other. The picture of Anna was folded out of view and Auntie put the paper behind her back. Nicholas did not object, as he found it difficult to read Danish. Anna breathed again and gently unclasped her hands. Whatever had come over Auntie?

As Anna was wondering about this the waiter came in with their last dinner. The chicken looked delicious, and Nicholas and Anna had a leg each. Anna struggled with her knife and fork, but Nicholas settled for fingers, and picked the leg up and tore at it with his teeth.

'Typical table manners of Tarzan, son of the apes,' thought Anna.

Auntie made sure they had as much as they wanted, and ordered extra chocolate sauce for the ice-cream. When they had all finished Auntie took a deep breath and turned to the children.

'Now I was intending to take you to Tivoli,' she said. 'As you know, they have roundabouts there and a switchback. I personally do not care much for roundabouts, as they make me feel giddy, and on the switchback I get sick.'

'What a shame, Auntie, the switchback is the greatest fun of all,' Nicholas said apprehensively.

He did not want to go to Tivoli at all, he wanted to stay at home with Danny, but he could not very well be so absurd as to say that switchbacks weren't fun.

'Of course there are other things worth seeing at Tivoli,' Auntie continued. 'There is the puppet theatre, for example.'

'But the switchback is much more fun,' Nicholas said staunchly, yet he wondered how he could say after that that he didn't want to go on the switchback at all that evening.

'I think they used to sell candyfloss at Tivoli too, but that only spoils your teeth,' Auntie went on. 'And it doesn't taste very nice either.'

'No, but it is fun to eat,' Anna said, which was true, after all.

'But you have just had such a lot of good things to eat,' Auntie said reproachfully, 'so we wouldn't go there just for the sake of the candyfloss. The only really amusing thing at Tivoli is the flea circus, but I suppose you have seen that before.'

'No, we haven't,' Nicholas said. 'I have never seen a flea in my life.'

'That is not really worth seeing either. It is just some small creatures pulling tiny little carriages and balancing along on a thread, I believe. That is all I can remember about Tivoli – I can't really see why it is so famous. Perhaps you don't want to go?'

Nicholas and Anna looked at each other. How could they be so rude as to tell Auntie that they didn't want to go, when she was so kindly inviting them?

'Well, of course we want to . . .' Nicholas said doubtfully.

'Thank you, Auntie, that would be very nice . . .' Anna started and then fell silent.

Auntie sighed.

'Unfortunately we can't go – Tivoli has not opened for the season yet. It doesn't open until 1 May. I just found out from the paper. I can't tell you how sorry I am to have to disappoint you.'

Auntie look miserably from Nicholas to Anna.

At last they understood.

'It doesn't matter, Auntie,' said Anna gaily. 'It doesn't matter one little bit!'

'Never mind,' Nicholas said, 'I don't want to go to Tivoli.'

'We can do that some other time,' Anna added.

'I've been on a switchback hundreds of times,' Nicholas continued, 'and the one in Stockholm is probably a thousand times better.'

'Roundabouts are only for babies.'

'And puppet theatres too.'

'Candyfloss only makes you sticky.'

'And who wants fleas, anyway?' Nicholas murmured.

'I would rather go to bed early,' Anna said, 'so that I feel really fresh for travelling tomorrow.'

'So would I,' Nicholas added and gave Auntie a hearty thump on the back. 'I'm glad we don't have to go out on the razzle again!'

Auntie seemed quite overcome. Finally she said:

'It really is noble of you to take it like this. I was

afraid you would both start crying. After all, the visit to Tivoli was going to be the best part of the whole visit to Copenhagen.'

'It could never have been that,' Nicholas assured her. 'I know something much better.'

'Whatever can that be?'

'We'll tell you that when we get home, Auntie,' Anna said quickly.

Auntie and the Laughter in the Wardrobe

The first thing Aunt Tina did the next day was to write a final postcard to Stockholm. She wrote:

My Dears,

Something terrible happened yesterday – Tivoli was closed! We could not go, and to cap all I read in the paper that a certain Anna Nielsen had won the pony in the Zoo lottery. What a near thing! The children might have won. Just imagine, even the name of the girl was almost the same! But I managed to prevent them from reading about the wretched business. The little dears pretended that they did not want to go to Tivoli at all, and went to bed like lambs. Now we are going out to buy souvenirs. We shall probably be back home before you get this card.

Your devoted Tina

That was what Auntie thought on Saturday.

She got dressed at a leisurely pace and rang the cashier to ask for the bill. At the same time she asked him to get a porter to fetch their luggage in time for the train, and then she rang Nicholas and Anna to tell them what she had arranged.

'Perhaps you had better pack your things as soon as possible,' she suggested. 'Then we will have the rest of the day free for shopping.'

'Yes, we'll do that,' Nicholas replied. 'We'll come in to you as soon as we are finished, Auntie; wait for us.'

Then he put the receiver down and said:

'Now comes the difficult part. How on earth are we going to pack Danny?'

Anna stared at him. She said she had planned for Danny to travel in the guard's van.

'Stupid!' Nicholas exclaimed. 'Where do we get the money for a goods ticket?'

Anna tried to think of a better idea. Perhaps they could cover him with a blanket again, and lead him down to the station if they were careful.

'Stupid!' said Nicholas again. 'There is always a doorman by the hotel entrance. Do you think he'll let us go off with the hotel blankets?'

He was right of course. The blankets were all marked with the name King Frederick. The doorman would know at once where they came from. But perhaps they could find an emergency exit to lead Danny out through – one that was not guarded. Once they got him out, they could tie him to some lamp-post near the station until it was time to smuggle him on to the train, through the turnstile.

'Stupid!' Nicholas said for the third time. 'How could we do that? Horses can't go through a turnstile, they would have to be folded in the middle first.'

Anna was getting tired of Nicholas.

'You think of something yourself, then,' she said. 'You have got all day. I'll tell Auntie that you want to shop alone, and she and I can go together. The train doesn't leave until tonight. Stupid yourself!'

Nicholas looked surprised for a moment, but soon collected himself.

'All right, you go,' he said. 'I'll fix Danny!'

He opened the window to let out the stable smells and opened the cupboard door to let Danny out. It was his turn to clean up.

Anna hurried in to Auntie.

Auntie was reading the paper, but quickly put it away when Anna came in.

'How much money have you left to buy presents with?' Auntie asked.

Anna opened her purse slowly and looked inside it to gain time. She only had a Danish coin worth a few pennies and the other ticket for the Zoo lottery.

'That's not much,' Auntie said. 'I told you it was silly to waste money on lottery tickets. But I'll tell you what we can do: I'll buy the ticket from you, and then you'll have a crown each again. I can keep the ticket, and if there is any prize, I'll get it instead.'

'I shouldn't think there will be a prize. They have already had the draw, and I would have known.'

'Maybe,' said Auntie, 'but I'll take that risk, as you were so good yesterday and didn't make a fuss about Tivoli. Tell me when you have decided what to buy, and I will pay with the ticket-money.'

How kind Auntie was! Anna took her by the arm and patted her coat sleeve as they walked along. She glanced at the doorman in the hotel entrance, and, sure enough, he was standing right in the middle of the doorway making himself look big just where Danny would have had to pass. However, Anna decided to forget all her worries for a while. After all, the train was not due to leave for a long time yet.

They went to a wonderful big shop called 'The Permanent Art Exhibition'. Auntie was going to buy presents there to take home to her friends.

The shop looked like an enormous glass aquarium, all made of windows.

Auntie bought a lovely midnight-blue dress with a pattern of northern lights on it for herself, and a cheese-cutter for her best friend. Anna found a little wooden stork's nest that she wanted, and a red soldier with a bearskin for Nicholas. Auntie paid for them.

After that they went to a shop where you could buy Danish porcelain. Auntie bought herself a blue teapot, and a vase for the children's parents. In the meantime Anna had found an ash-tray with Hans Andersen's little mermaid on it for her father, and two small porcelain birds in blue for her mother. Auntie paid for those too.

They went to a large sweet-shop to buy sweets. Anna chose a golden box of cat's tongues made of chocolate. This she insisted on giving to Aunt Tina for being so kind and taking them with her to Denmark. Auntie said that Anna's one crown would pay for that too.

They had taken a very long time over their shopping, and now it was high time to go home. Anna was worried about Danny again. She couldn't believe that Nicholas had arranged everything for the best. She felt she must hurry home and find out what he had done.

'Now pack carefully so that nothing gets broken,' Auntie said as they parted outside their hotel rooms.

Anna just nodded. She thought she could hear Danny kicking in the cupboard, although he should have been gone from there long ago.

'Well, what have you planned for us to do?' Anna asked when she saw Nicholas and Danny exactly where she had left them.

Nicholas looked stubborn.

'We can't get Danny out through the emergency exit, because there is a fire-escape ladder there, and horses can't climb,' Nicholas said. 'And we can't creep down the main staircase when nobody is looking, because horses can't walk *down* stairs, they can only walk up. He won't do it. We'll have to put him in Auntie's trunk.'

Now it was Anna's turn to sniff contemptuously.

'Stupid!' she exclaimed. 'Surely you realize that that won't work!'

'Oh yes, it will,' said Nicholas. 'I have tried it.'

Anna laughed crossly. Certainly Auntie's trunk was the bulkiest she had ever seen – Auntie liked her dresses to travel hanging up, they must not get the slightest bit crushed, and the trunk looked like a little wardrobe – but all the same . . .

'I suppose you have asked Auntie if you can borrow it?' she asked in her most annoying voice.

'No, but I have been out finding boxes to put Auntie's things in so that they get to Stockholm too,' Nicholas said coolly.

He patted Danny on the muzzle.

'Stand still here, Danny, and be quiet, we must just go in to Auntie and have a look at something,' he said, and closed the cupboard door.

Just then Auntie came in.

'Now I'd like to see if you have packed everything,' she said. 'The porter will soon be here and then all the bags must be ready.'

Nicholas and Anna were taken so much by surprise that they could think of nothing to say. If she had come in only a few seconds earlier, she would have seen Danny – all of him.

'Where are your suitcases?' Auntie asked.

Anna hurriedly dragged them out from under a bed. Fortunately Nicholas had packed them. It looked as if he had tossed everything in with a spade and then jumped on top to get the cases shut, but all their things were there.

'What a way to pack!' Auntie exclaimed. 'Why can't Mummy teach you to use suitcases that are big enough? It wouldn't cost you any more, and think of the advantage of getting everything in easily. Well, we can't do anything about it now.'

'I'll bring huge trunks next time,' Nicholas said helpfully. 'I promise I will, Auntie!'

There was a neighing sound from the cupboard.

Auntie hardly looked surprised at all to start with. Then she slowly turned round.

'What was that?' she asked.

Nicholas and Anna could not reply.

Auntie looked at the cupboard.

'Who on earth can be laughing in that strange way in the cupboard?' she asked.

Nicholas and Anna had no answer this time either. They were hoping that Auntie would not believe her ears if they said nothing about the whole business. But Auntie took a step towards the cupboard. Nicholas collected himself with a tremendous effort.

'It is only the hall porter,' he said.

'The hall porter? The porter!!! What in heaven's name is he doing in your cupboard?' she exclaimed.

'He probably has some little job to do,' Nicholas tried.

Auntie snorted.

'In the pitch dark? What sort of pleasure would that give him? What a terrible laugh! It sounded just like the neighing of a horse. What does that fellow mean by sitting in the cupboard, laughing?'

'Perhaps he is not sitting, he may be standing,' Nicholas suggested.

Auntie looked at him as if she had never seen him before. She didn't seem to think that his suggestion really improved the situation.

'If it *is* the hall porter, he must be mad,' Auntie decided. 'What kind of hotel is this? He must get out of there at once. Tell him so!'

She tried to approach the door, but Anna stood in the way.

'Please, Auntie, we can't do that,' she said. 'Don't disturb him. It's not our cupboard, after all, it belongs to the hotel.'

'What nonsense! If we've paid for the room, we have a right to the cupboard as well, and he need not think that I intend to put up with his ridiculous neighing. Let me past!'

Nicholas went and stood next to Anna in front of the cupboard.

'Don't open the door, Auntie, perhaps he is counting the hangers in there, or maybe he wants to be in peace and quiet to work out how many rooms are vacant today ... so that he knows what to answer when people ring up.'

'Well, they won't ring him up in the cupboard, will they?' Auntie said angrily. 'I've never heard such a ridiculous idea! You really are terrible children for contradicting. One would have to look far and wide to find anything to beat such pig-headedness. I am beginning to understand how your father got his grey hairs and all those wrinkles in his forehead.'

'But Daddy has said that one should not disturb people one doesn't know,' Nicholas went on stubbornly. He kept his hands behind his back, realizing that he would have to start fingering the key in a casual sort of way if he was going to manage to turn it and get it out before Auntie reached the door. Anna tried to help. She grabbed Auntie by the arm.

'Come on, don't let's take any notice of him,' she begged. 'We can pretend we didn't hear, then he'll soon go away. Look, from this window you can see the dairy I went past yesterday. You can see it much better from this window.'

Auntie shook herself free. She was getting more and more angry.

'Dairy this and dairy that! I don't know how long you talked about that wretched shop yesterday. What is all this unhealthy nonsense about dairies? Surely you are not a baby any longer, Anna?'

She went resolutely back to the cupboard and pushed Nicholas aside. But the key was gone. Auntie took a step backwards.

'Now I understand it all,' she said looking at the children. 'He's drunk, of course, and he has gone in there to sleep it off. And he has taken the key with him.'

Auntie knocked at the door.

'Hey, you in there, come out at once!'

When she said that Danny neighed again.

'Please leave him alone,' Anna and Nicholas both implored her with their most coaxing voices.

Auntie looked at them thoughtfully.

'You are too young to understand this,' she said finally. 'I shall speak to the hotel manager. You go into my room in the meantime and stay there.'

Auntie walked briskly to the telephone and lifted the receiver. But there was no list to give her the number of the hotel manager.

'Inefficient!' she snapped as she pushed the children in front of her out of the room.

She left them in her room with a warning:

'Don't go back in there while I am away. You never know *what* drunken people might get up to. I shall be back immediately.'

She hurried off down the corridor.

Nicholas and Anna stood for a moment as if struck by lightning. But then they both pulled themselves together.

'They are not going to touch our very own pony!' Nicholas said.

'Let's rescue him into this room for the time being, and after that we'll see,' Anna said hurriedly.

They both rushed back to their room.

Danny was delighted to get out of the cupboard. He capered wildly in the corridor and kicked for joy in Auntie's room.

'Darling Danny! You are as pretty as a kitten and a squirrel and Audrey Hepburn all at once! We must get you home somehow,' Anna murmured.

'Don't stand there being soppy!' Nicholas told her. 'Auntie will soon be back – she is hot on our trail . . .'

'What shall we do then?' Anna asked helplessly.

'Put him in Auntie's trunk, as I said,' Nicholas whispered. 'Get her things out quickly – shove them all in the wardrobe.'

They rushed over to the trunk and opened it wide. What a terrible lot of clothes Auntie had brought just for one week! They grabbed an armful each and then came back for odds and ends several times. It seemed to take ages before everything was stowed away in the cupboard. And now for Danny – what luck that the trunk was so big!

'Look how good he is, going in without a murmur,' Anna said as she led Danny into the trunk. 'My poor, very own pony!'

What a terrible lot of clothes Auntie had brought just for one week!

'He is mine just as much,' Nicholas protested. 'Get out of the way so that I can close the trunk. I must make some holes too, so that he can breathe.'

Nicholas got some scissors out of the desk and set to work making a hole in a corner of the trunk. He would have to buy Auntie another one with his pocket-money eventually. Time enough to worry about that later.

'You did clean up in the cupboard, I hope?' Anna said breathlessly.

'Yes, but of course there is a bit of a smell still.'

They both stared at the closed door as if they were trying to see what was going to happen in the next room.

There was a knock at the door.

'I am from the Railways. There is a trunk to be called for here, is there?' a porter said to Anna when she opened the door.

Anna felt like clapping her hands.

'Do come in! The trunk is here. You take it, it's all ready!'

The porter came in and lifted one end of the trunk.

'It's quite a weight, isn't it? What could be inside, I wonder?'

'Well,' said Nicholas, 'it belongs to the animal kingdom and begins with the letter P, that I can tell you. But don't try to guess, we haven't time. We have a train to catch!'

Auntie is Made to Vibrate

'Go with him to the station, so you see where he puts it,' Anna whispered to Nicholas. 'I'll tell Auntie that you have gone ahead.'

Nicholas looked scared. He was afraid that he would not be able to manage alone, but Anna gave him a shove.

'It says on the ticket which train we are getting. The porter is sure to know the way. You must let Danny out as soon as you get on the train, otherwise it is cruelty to animals, you see.'

Nicholas rushed after the porter, who had already disappeared round the corner with the trunk on his little trolley.

Anna sighed with relief and went back to her room. She had to see how Auntie was getting on.

Auntie was standing in front of the open cupboard together with an elegant fat gentleman and the large porter from the reception desk.

'Oh yes, he did!' Auntie was saying as Anna came in. 'I heard him myself, sitting in there laughing. I don't care if a thousand witnesses saw him in reception; somebody was in here, and that's a fact. And don't interrupt me, I tell you! *I* am the one who does the talking. How can we ever hope to clear up Danish-Swedish relationships and inter-Scandinavian collaboration and friendship and understanding across the seas if any hotel porter who chooses can sit and laugh in one's cupboards, just like that? The children were terrified!'

'Excuse me . . .' said the porter.

'There must be some misunderstanding,' said the hotel manager.

'And I don't want to be interrupted either,' Auntie continued. 'I want all this cleared up before the man comes to fetch our luggage.'

'He *has* already,' Anna said.

'Good!' said the hotel manager.

Auntie wheeled round.

She grabbed the children's suitcases and threw

'Oh yes, he did!' Auntie was saying . . .

a commanding glance towards the hotel manager.

'Stay here!' she ordered.

Anna would never have believed that their gentle little Aunt Tina could be so terrifying. Furiously she stalked off to her own room and looked round for the porter. Anna followed her and helped her to look, although she would have preferred to keep out of the way.

'He has taken the trunk already,' she explained.

'But my dear child, of course he was meant to take your suitcases as well,' cried Auntie.

She surveyed the room again and flung open the door of the wardrobe to make sure that nothing had been forgotten. What luck that Danny was not standing in there, Anna thought.

'Never in all my life . . . what on *earth* is this supposed to mean . . .? All the things that were in the trunk, lying here in a dreadful muddle!'

Anna gasped for breath.

'It was . . . we . . . Nicholas and I took those things out,' she finally managed to say. 'The porter never said he was to take the clothes . . . we thought he only had to take the trunk . .'

Auntie said nothing at all. She pursed her lips and gazed at Anna so hard that it almost hurt.

'Don't say any more, Auntie,' Anna begged. 'Please, Auntie, or we'll miss the train.'

This put life into Auntie.

'To miss the train, that would be the last straw,' she hissed. 'Go to your room and make sure you haven't forgotten your toothbrush . . . I must find something to put my clothes in, and ring for a taxi.'

'I know where there are some boxes,' Anna told her. She rushed off and fetched all the boxes that Nicholas had hidden behind his bed. Auntie was pleasantly surprised to see them. She didn't have time to ask where Anna had managed to find the boxes in such a hurry.

Then they both started packing with frantic haste. There seemed to be twice as many dresses now that they were all in one heap and things seemed to bulge and overflow from all the boxes. Auntie put everything in higgledy-piggledy and flung the dresses from box to box. You might almost have said that she was chucking them around and cramming and shoving and squashing them if she hadn't been such a refined aunt. Anna thought that Auntie was probably swearing under her breath too, although she was too well-mannered to show it. At last they were sitting in the taxi.

Anna dared not look at Auntie.

'We forgot to say good-bye to the hotel manager and the porter,' she whispered. 'They are still standing outside our wardrobe.'

'Let them stand there,' Auntie snapped coldly.

As soon as the taxi drew up at the station Auntie started worrying about Nicholas, as she was in a worrying mood anyway. Anna was worried too, but she dared not show it. She had to be steady and cheerful all the time to keep Auntie calm.

'Nicholas is so sensible,' Anna said, 'or at least he will be when he grows up, Mummy says. I wouldn't be a bit surprised if sense hasn't broken out now, while we were in Denmark.'

'I'd like to see that sense before I can believe in it,' Auntie sighed wearily.

She really seemed worn out now. Almost as though she found it troublesome to look after children for a whole week. As if looking after children were anything to complain about, thought Anna. She ought to try looking after a secret pony!

'My nerves will soon break completely,' Anna said to herself, but Auntie heard and looked at her quite kindly.

'Mine are completely worn out,' Auntie said. 'Nothing but shreds left. I shall have to have a rest-cure when I get home.'

Anna patted Auntie's hand.

Crowds of people were hurrying to and fro. Some stood by high brass-topped trolleys drinking beer out of glass mugs in the middle of the main hall of the station, while others hurried about with suitcases. There were queues of people by the souvenir shop buying last-minute presents. Nicholas was nowhere to be seen. Auntie groaned.

'If he doesn't come at once, I shall scream!'

Anna looked round desperately.

She caught sight of a strange contraption that looked rather like a weighing-machine. It consisted of an iron platform for standing on and in front of it was a high pillar made of metal, with a slot to put coins in.

'Put coin in here,' it said. 'The automatic machine will vibrate away all your tiredness. No dangerous radiation, no electric shocks. Try it for yourself!'

Anna gently led Auntie up to the machine.

'Stand here, Auntie dear,' she said; 'you will see how much better you feel!'

Anna quickly brought out her last Danish coin – as Auntie had paid for everything she still had it in her purse – and pressed it into the slot. Auntie was just about to ask what it was all about, when the machine started. The little iron footplate began jumping and shaking under her feet so violently that the sand and grit in the grooves of the plate began to bounce up in the air. Auntie opened her mouth as if to shout for help and grabbed hold of the machine, but she did not actually step off. Anna watched her carefully to see what effect the treatment was having. Auntie was shaking so that her nylon stockings quivered on her legs and her coat flapped violently. You could see that the vibrations continued right up to Auntie's head, because her earrings were waving about and her hat was wobbling. Suddenly Auntie took a violent jump into the air and landed next to Anna.

'Did it make you feel better so quickly?' Anna said, feeling very pleased, and then she stepped up on the machine to take Auntie's place.

It tickled under her feet, and her knees felt rather funny, but she didn't have time to feel anything else because now Auntie really did scream.

'Nicholas!' she yelled so that the whole station echoed.

'Here I am,' said Nicholas appearing suddenly out of the crowd.

He looked so cheerful and happy as he gave Auntie a hug that she stopped screaming at once.

'Don't worry, everything is fine. I just saw the trunk on to the train.'

Auntie and Anna both looked relieved. The train was due to leave in three minutes and Auntie dragged them off to the platform at once. Anna barely had time to whisper to Nicholas:

'How did it go?'

And he just had time to answer:

'Fine. The train was not in when we got here, so I

stayed by myself with the trunk in a left-luggage place. I let him out for a few minutes and we walked up and down behind a rack of luggage. Now he is back in the trunk.'

'Did he neigh at all?'

'No, he only snorted. I told the porter I was a ventriloquist.'

'Did he believe you?'

'No. "Come off it!" he said. "That's the engine letting off steam." '

Nicholas laughed at the thought of it.

Auntie hurried them on and they half ran down the platform along the great Stockholm express.

'Here we are!' Nicholas shouted and climbed into a carriage. Anna followed him and squeezed her way along the corridor. They stopped by their compartment, a sleeper with nicely made-up bunks, and Auntie's large trunk taking up nearly all the floor-space. Anna patted it lovingly.

'We managed to catch the train after all, in spite of our thousand-and-one troubles,' Auntie sighed.

At that moment the train started to move.

The Whistle Blows and the Train Departs

'It's going to be wonderful to get to bed,' Auntie sighed, and dropped some of her boxes on top of the trunk.

'I bags the top bunk!' Nicholas shouted.

'I bags the middle one!' Anna shouted.

'I bags the bottom one,' Auntie said kindly.

'How can you, Auntie, surely that's not a bit exciting?'

'That's exactly why,' Auntie replied. 'I'm not one for excitement, I can tell you. It only gives you goose-pimples and makes you sleep badly at night.'

Nicholas and Anna laughed. But then the same thought occurred to them both: if Auntie had the bottom bunk she would be nearest to the trunk. Then how would they be able to get Danny out without waking her?

'No ... come to think of it, don't let's count that. We'll start again. I bags the *bottom* bunk!'

'And I the middle one,' Anna said quickly. 'Then you'll have the top one, Auntie.'

Auntie looked astonished.

'But you two are always fighting about who is to sleep in the top bunk. Surely I can't –'

'Yes, you can, Auntie,' Nicholas said generously. 'I am tired of sleeping in the top one. I have grown out of it. Nowadays I like the bottom bunk much better.'

'Well, I must say that is a quick development. If you gain so much in age and wisdom in a couple of minutes we shall all have white hair by the time we get home. What is the point of all this?'

'Nothing, Auntie. It's just that I would feel so much safer with you at the top.'

'In what way?' Auntie wondered.

'Well ... I don't know ... it's just how I feel. If a tunnel were to collapse on top of the train or something.'

'Then I would take the first blow, you mean. Thank you very much.'

'I'm afraid of sleeping up there,' Nicholas went on. 'I might dream that I'm jumping off the Eiffel Tower and fall down and hurt myself.'

'And I've got terrible growing-pains in my legs, so I can't climb up there,' Anna added hastily.

'All right, all right, I don't wish to hear any more about your aches and pains. Do as you like,' Auntie said at last. 'I have never known such contrary children. But if you think I am going to run up and down like a spider on a thread once I've got to bed, to give you glasses of water and tuck you in every other minute, you are very much mistaken ... And you mustn't lie down here talking, either, if that's what you were planning.'

'Oh no, we'll be absolutely quiet so that you can go to sleep at once,' Nicholas promised.

'Off you go into the corridor, then, while I get undressed!'

She pushed them both out and closed the sliding door behind them. Auntie was alone with the trunk.

Anna and Nicholas pressed their ears against the door to try to hear what was going on, but the train was making too much noise. All they could make out was the clatter of the wheels, which seemed to be saying 'to-Stockholm-to-Stockholm-to-Stockholm . . .' A man looked out of a door farther down the corridor. Anna and Nicholas quickly straightened themselves up.

'It's probably only about six hundred and thirty-two kilometres to Stockholm now,' Nicholas said hopefully. 'I'll have a look in my pocket diary.'

'Did you have time to buy anything for Mummy and Daddy?' Anna asked.

'No. I had to pay the porter with my Swedish ten-crown note. The trunk was so heavy he asked me if I had removed the paving-stones round the Town Hall to take home.'

Anna sighed. 'My things will have to be from both of us, then, I suppose.'

She tried to hear what Auntie was doing without turning her head. Just then the door opened and Auntie put out her pale refined hand from the top bunk. She was already in bed, dressed in her violet-coloured bed-jacket with a bow.

'I couldn't be bothered to move everything from the boxes into the trunk,' she said. 'It's too cramped in here. We will fix that in the morning, somehow.'

Nicholas and Anna shuddered. They came in and shut the door quickly. They did not have time to put up the cloth screens beside their bunks or to play with the little lamps above the beds that looked like shiny cigarette-cases. They just wanted to get to bed quickly so that Auntie could go to sleep. Anna climbed up into her bunk and undressed lying down rather like an athletic eel. Nicholas stood on the patch of floor between the trunk and the door and tore off his clothes in no time. As each garment came off he flung it into the net by his bunk. They turned off the light at once and counted to one hundred.

'Are you asleep, Aunt Tina?' Anna whispered.

'No, I'm lying thinking about everything that has happened to us, all our adventures. How Anna got lost at the Zoo and Nicholas at the Glyptotek Museum. And the grass you picked for Anna, Nicholas. And that fellow in the cupboard. There is one thing I cannot understand . . .'

'What is that?' Nicholas and Anna whispered.

'Why Tivoli doesn't open until May,' Auntie replied and turned over in her bunk.

'Go to sleep now, Auntie,' Nicholas told her sternly.

Auntie chuckled a little. It sounded as though she were laughing as she said good night. Anna put her hand under the pillow where it felt nice and cool, and counted to a hundred three more times. What would happen if Auntie were one of those people who can't sleep in trains and who just lie there thinking all night? But she slept so well on the way to Copenhagen, surely she could sleep on the way back to Stockholm too? Anna counted two hundred more and then she heard Nicholas breathing in her ear.

'I'm going to open the trunk now. I can't wait any longer.'

Anna peeped down at him in the dark. They switched on the night-light for a moment to find the locks of the trunk, then switched it off again. They managed to open the trunk a little but not enough for Danny to get out. Nicholas closed the lid again.

'We'll have to pull it out into the corridor,' he whispered.

That was easier said than done. Danny was heavy and the trunk was large. It was difficult to get hold of, and there was nowhere to stand as you pulled it along.

Nicholas had to climb into the narrow space between the trunk and the window and, bracing himself against the trunk, push for all he was worth with hands and feet. The trunk moved a couple of inches unwillingly.

'Hehehehee!' neighed Danny suddenly.

Nicholas and Anna stood absolutely still in the dark, holding their breath. But apparently Auntie had heard nothing. She must be fast asleep.

'We'll have to fix matters outside in the corridor,' Nicholas whispered. 'This doesn't work.'

Anna climbed down, opened the door and peeped out. No one was about. They had to try at once. With a tremendous effort they managed to get the trunk into the corridor.

'We are just moving things around a bit in here,' Nicholas explained to a man who was passing their compartment.

The man looked a little annoyed when he had to climb over the trunk but he said nothing and disappeared down the other end of the train. Nicholas and Anna continued with their struggle.

'Now we can open the trunk if nobody is coming,' Anna gasped at last.

They looked up and down the corridor. No one was about, so Anna opened the trunk and let Danny out. Nicholas grabbed the empty trunk and heaved it on to Anna's bed.

'There! Now Danny can stand on the floor next to us. Auntie won't notice anything until tomorrow. In you go. Danny! Back, back, back!'

Danny was not keen on being shut up again in the dark compartment, but when Nicholas scratched his head and Anna patted his flank on the right, as they had been told to do, he backed in. They closed the door quietly. Nothing more need happen until the morning, they thought.

Anna brought Danny's nosebag out of her suitcase. There was not much food left now, in spite of the grass Nicholas had picked. There were only a few rusks and pieces of bread in the bag. She took a rusk and felt for Danny's muzzle in the dark. Danny found her hand and started munching the rusk. Suddenly a train going in the other direction screamed past with a shrill whistle. Danny snorted and dropped the rusk, but Nicholas found it for him.

'Here you are, this is the last piece,' he whispered.

Auntie stirred in her bunk.

'What are you munching down there, children?' she asked sleepily. 'You should never eat after cleaning your teeth, you know.'

Anna held Danny's muzzle to stop him chewing. 'Nothing, Auntie,' she said.

'I'm not eating either,' Nicholas assured her. 'Shall I climb up and show you that my mouth is empty?'

'No, thank you. Don't put yourself out, just go to sleep,' Auntie replied.

Nicholas's and Anna's hearts started beating again. They tried to be even more quiet. They both patted Danny to keep him from making any more noise before Auntie had gone to sleep once more. At last Anna leaned over and whispered to Nicholas:

'We can't stand here all night. I want to go to bed. Give Danny a drink in case his mouth is dry after the rusk, and then we'll go to sleep.'

They felt their way to the basin and lifted up the wooden cover. Then Nicholas pressed the cold tap while Anna held on to Danny.

'There now, come and have a drink from the basin, little fellow,' she murmured.

But then Auntie came to again.

'What is this I hear? Is Nicholas trying to drink from the basin? It's out of the question. Under *no* circumstances . . .' she said sharply.

Nicholas looked up. He couldn't see Auntie's face. She seemed to be lying with her back to them, listening.

'No, no, no. I am not going to do that, Auntie! You just go to sleep!'

It was quite fun that Auntie was so near to discovering Danny, because she never actually did.

'Stop, you're putting your whole head in, you silly!' Anna whispered.

Danny snorted cheerfully.

'Oh dear, what a cold you've got, Anna,' came Auntie's voice from above. 'Get that spare blanket and put it on your bed at once.'

'Yes, Auntie, I have already done that. Now do go to sleep, Auntie dear!'

Aunt Tina sighed. Anna tried to push Danny away from the basin so that he would not get water in his ears, but he had decided to be difficult and would not budge. He pushed his head against the tap so that water sprayed out on one side.

'Take him away, I'm getting soaked!' Nicholas whispered.

Anna scratched Danny's head and patted him on the right flank again.

'There, there, aren't you sweet!' Nicholas said encouragingly.

'You like it when I scratch your ear, don't you?' Anna whispered.

Danny sighed happily.

'Now I've just about had enough!' Auntie's voice snapped sharply. And she did not sound sleepy any longer. 'Stop scratching each other's ears and fooling about down there! It's the middle of the night, after all. And don't you dare imitate that ridiculous porter's silly neighing. You'll wake everybody up. Do you hear?'

'Oh yes, Auntie. We are asleep now,' Nicholas answered, and made a snoring noise.

They crept into the bottom bunk and lay stock still. They were afraid it might occur to Auntie to look down. What did a pony look like from above in the dark? Perhaps he couldn't be seen at all, or maybe he was clearly visible . . .

Anna murmured to Nicholas:

'We can't go on like this. We'll have to take him outside in the corridor. Everybody must have gone to bed by now.'

'All right,' Nicholas replied.

He looked up towards Auntie, but she could not be heard or seen. Then he quickly opened the door. 'I am just going to the lavatory,' he said, and pulled Danny into the corridor with him.

Good Night?

The corridor of the train was empty as far as the eye could see. The train shook and rattled, and outside the windows the night flickered past like an endlessly long blue scarf. In places there were moving flashes from the headlamps of cars and rows of twinkling lights. It was pretty and exciting at the same time. Never before had Nicholas been alone with a pony in the corridor of a train. He decided to take advantage of the opportunity.

'We might as well go for a ride,' he thought. 'You need exercise, Danny, and I'll have to learn to ride as soon as possible. Keep still for a moment!'

Danny had only a halter on, there was no saddle or blanket to sit on, but Nicholas did not mind riding bareback. Danny was so small, anyway, that one could sit on his back and almost touch the ground with one's feet. Riding him could not be very dangerous.

'Wait a little! Whoa there!'

Nicholas managed to scramble up on to Danny's back. It was comfortable and felt pleasantly warm and steady. Nicholas decided that he would ride to school on Danny every morning. Or every other morning at least, if Anna insisted on riding too.

'Come along, Danny, off you go!' Nicholas said as he pressed his knees against the sides of the pony.

Danny set off at a gallop. For a long time he had been waiting for a chance to stretch and run. He rushed on as far as he could but he had to stop at the end of the carriage. This made him kick angrily. If there had been room Nicholas would have fallen off, but there wasn't, so he just bumped into the wall.

'Oh, dear, what if someone heard us! We had better go on into the next carriage,' he thought.

He stretched out his arm and pushed open the swing-door. Danny pricked up his ears at the sight of the shaking passageway linking the two carriages but then he put one hoof forward and bravely tested it. 'There's a good chap! You clever horse!' Nicholas murmured encouragingly and they were soon over in the next carriage and off again. Nobody was about here either, but just to be on the safe side Nicholas dismounted at each new carriage and peeped in before riding on. He was surprisingly lucky, but unfortunately there were not many carriages left before they reached the engine. Both Nicholas and Danny wanted to go on.

'We'll turn here and ride back in the other direction,' Nicholas decided.

But this was not as easy as he imagined. Although Danny was small it was still difficult to turn him round in the narrow corridor. Nicholas had to get down and pull him by his mane. He was going to try to persuade Danny to bend in the middle just enough to turn, but Danny refused, so in the end Nicholas had to push him backwards down a whole carriage until he came to a place where the corridor was a little wider. He opened the door of the lavatory and pushed the back part of Danny in there. After that it was easy to turn him round. Danny sighed. Walking backwards had made him impatient. Nicholas remounted.

'Gee-up, gee-up! Off we go!' Nicholas commanded and pressed with his knees, which he thought was the right thing to do.

But then Danny bucked. He kicked hard at a door behind them and flung his head forward so that Nicholas nearly fell off. But he did not budge from the spot.

The door behind them opened and an angry head appeared. It belonged to a pyjama-clad body somewhere in the middle bunk. The man immediately spotted Nicholas and Danny.

'What do you mean by kicking my door in the middle of the night and . . .!' he shouted.

Then his voice changed and he sounded different but just as angry.

'What on . . . a whole horse to kick around with? Aren't you ashamed of yourself, child? Is there no guard . . .?'

When Danny heard the angry voice behind him he suddenly came to life.

'Run for all you are worth!' Nicholas whispered and Danny rushed off into the next carriage as fast as his little legs would carry him. They continued on into the one after that without stopping, but there Nicholas wanted to halt for a moment to see if anyone was about. He grabbed hold of the halter and tried to brake with his feet. Then Danny kicked again. He hit another door and Nicholas heard it open slowly. After that Nicholas decided to let Danny keep running.

'Look, Mummy, what a sweet little horse,' a sleepy child's voice said behind him, and an even sleepier mother replied:

'Dog, you mean. Now close the door at once and go back to bed!'

Danny galloped out of earshot with clattering hooves. Fortunately the clattering of the train was even louder.

'Run for all you are worth!' Nicholas whispered

Nicholas realized that he would have to find their compartment and hide Danny away, but he could not remember the number. How far had he ridden? Four carriages there and two back? Or was it three? He thought he had found the right place and opened a door. It was the wrong one. He caught sight of a woman's head covered with curlers.

'I'm terribly sorry. I didn't mean to wake you!' he stammered. 'I thought it was my compartment.'

'Your compartment? Can't you see that *I* am sleeping here? Then why do you come trailing here with dogs ... what's this I see? Goodness gracious, it's a horse! A horse! Do you think this is a horsebox?'

Nicholas closed the door as quickly as he could and let Danny gallop off. His compartment must be in the next carriage – compartment No. 26 or 38, he thought: but how should he dare to look and find out?

Anna had been lying still for an eternity, waiting for Nicholas to return. She dared not go out for fear of Auntie following her. Suddenly she heard galloping hooves outside, and then the sound died away again. There was a sharp knock at the door.

'Haven't you gone to sleep yet, children?' Auntie asked. 'Open the door for Nicholas. Surely he doesn't have to knock before coming in?'

Anna opened the door cautiously but shut it again quickly. It was not Nicholas but a guard.

'It's not Nicholas, Auntie – it's somebody else.'

Then Auntie turned into Aunt Tina the Terrible again. She was clearly getting into the habit.

'Who can it be?' she asked in a loud voice. 'I'll teach them to disturb old people and sleepless little children! Now, what is it all about?'

'I am sorry to disturb you, but we have had some

complaints from passengers . . .' the guard began, when Auntie opened the door.

'Complaints!' she exclaimed. 'Did you say complaints? Well, I am not surprised, the way you go around banging on doors. Is there an extra charge for going to sleep in express trains these days? What do you mean by waking us up like this? Is there going to be a derailment or something?'

'No, it's about a horse,' the guard said. 'Several of the passengers have been disturbed by a horse galloping along the corridor.'

'A horse!' Auntie cried. 'A horse in a train? That's the silliest thing I have heard for a long time. Are you really such a fool that you believe anything people tell you?'

'Well, no, that's just what I said, that it must be a mistake. "You must have dreamt it, sir," I said. "I haven't clipped a horse ticket for several years, and horses always travel in the goods van," I said . . .'

'There you are, then,' Auntie cried. 'Surely you don't have to come and wake decent people up in the middle of the night just to talk rubbish. Please go away at once and let us have some peace and quiet. As if it were not difficult enough to sleep in trains without having to hear about other people's dreadful nightmares . . .'

'Well, I'm very sorry, but I did promise to investigate,' the guard insisted.

Anna crept under the bedclothes and held them tightly over her head as she listened.

'No, *really*, I think I shall go crazy!' Auntie exclaimed. 'Do you seriously think that you are looking for a horse in here? Perhaps you have never seen a horse? Horses are six feet high with a big head at one end and a long tail at the other. Be good enough to hand me my dressing-gown so that I can descend and chase you out!'

Now the guard sounded like a patient mother:

'Please be calm, madam. This is just a routine investigation. I can see for myself that there is no horse in here.'

'Really!' Auntie continued. 'Are you sure you don't wish to look under the children's pillows to see if they may have hidden a horse there? Or in my toothbrush case, perhaps? Don't mind me!'

'There is no need to be so sarcastic, madam. I am only doing my duty. Good night!'

He closed the door with a bang and Anna peered out from under her sheet to make sure that he had really gone.

'Good night,' Auntie muttered from her bunk. 'A good night indeed! I have never known the like of it.'

'What a good thing you chased him away,' Anna whispered. 'I was so frightened!'

She got up hurriedly and opened the door enough to peep out. The guard was just disappearing down the corridor in the direction of the engine. He had decided to ask the angry man in the next carriage how sure he was that he had actually seen a horse. Anna looked round anxiously for Nicholas. First she saw only empty corridors but after a while she glimpsed him cautiously peeping round a corner at the other end of the carriage. As soon as he saw her he waved.

'What shall I do? He will find us,' he whispered as loudly as he dared.

Anna understood without actually hearing what he said.

She signalled to him to come closer.

Nicholas looked around and then approached stealthily with Danny behind him. Anna went up to Nicholas and whispered in his ear.

'Bring Danny back into our compartment. They won't look there again in a hurry. And if they do we'll have to confess everything.'

Nicholas nodded gloomily. Fearing the worst, Anna opened the sliding door and pushed Danny in.

'Has Nicholas gone to bed now?' Auntie inquired sharply.

'I'm just going now, Auntie,' Nicholas said.

The sliding door closed behind him and darkness engulfed them all once more.

'Bring Danny back into our compartment . . .'

Waking up

In some way or another they must have gone to sleep, for all of a sudden Anna felt herself waking up, and that meant she must have slept. It was much lighter on both sides of the blind. It was probably a fine day.

Danny stood with his head hanging low, rocking with the movements of the train. The green curtain by the window looked a little odd, as though Danny had been chewing it during the night. However, it was not torn, just rather wet. Anna peeped down at Nicholas. He was asleep. Auntie was breathing peacefully. If only she would go on until they reached Stockholm!

Anna was thinking. Who would wake them if she went to sleep again? The guard, of course. The guard had woken them on their way to Copenhagen. And the first thing he would see when he opened the door? Danny of course.

Anna turned over anxiously. What would happen then? Would he confiscate the pony, as teachers confiscated toys that should not have been brought to school? Or perhaps Auntie would have to pay a fine? Poor Auntie, who had done no wrong and who had no idea that she was breaking train regulations, or whatever they were called. It was always the adults who had to pay for the things children got up to – Anna remembered that from the time when Nicholas cut windows in the neighbour's hedge with Daddy's shears. As she had told him off about horses that didn't exist, the guard would probably be particularly nasty to Auntie if he found the horse in their compartment. Poor, dear Auntie! Anna felt like climbing up and patting her as she slept, although nothing had happened yet. Perhaps there would not be time afterwards when disaster had overtaken them.

'I had better put Danny out in the lavatory for the last part of the journey,' Anna thought.

She climbed down from her bunk as quietly as a mouse and managed to open the door without a sound. Even Danny did not move. 'Stay there,' she whispered. She crept out cautiously to make sure that nobody was about. She wanted to make sure the coast was clear; then she would come back for Danny. The train was shaking as she walked down the corridor. It was difficult for Anna to stand up, sleepy as she was, but at last she managed to get to the lavatory. It was empty and light in there.

When she came out she saw the guard walking past in the direction of the engine. Anna called out to him.

'Mr Guard! Excuse me . . .'

He stopped and turned round. Anna was rather embarrassed, but she was very anxious to find out what had happened.

'What did the man say who had seen a horse?' she asked.

The guard snorted angrily. He recognized her from last night.

'Nothing,' he said; 'he got off at Växjö.'

Anna smiled with relief. She tiptoed back to their compartment and stood there quietly until the guard had gone. Then she opened the door cautiously and patted Danny on his right flank until he turned his head, and then she led him out into the corridor. He looked lively and wide awake already.

She climbed down from her bunk . . .

'Dear Danny, we'll soon be home now, and then we'll show you what a nice place it is. I have a room of my own, and so has Nicholas, and we'll let you live in the garage for the time being ... but very soon we'll build you a proper stable. If Daddy will let us, that is!'

She took him along to the lavatory and gave him some water to drink from the basin. But when she tried to shut the door, she realized that it was impossible. The door opened inwards and took up a lot of space. It could not be shut with Danny inside, and to take him out and then shut the door was pointless ... Anna went cold with horror. What could she do now? Suddenly she had an idea. The last carriages of trains sometimes have a little platform at the end, like a small iron balcony, where you can stand and wave. There Danny could stand, and as ponies can't open gates or doors there would be no danger of him falling out.

'Come on, Danny, we'll have to hurry!' Anna ran as fast as she could through the corridors and Danny followed her happily. Just once they had to wait out of sight between two carriages for a man to go back into his compartment. They reached the little platform safely. It was terribly windy out there. Anna in her thin pyjamas pressed herself against Danny and tried to keep her hair from blowing about. Danny gasped for breath, but he looked quite contented.

'You must have your blanket over you here, otherwise you'll catch a cold,' Anna shouted – it was the only way to make herself heard.

Danny neighed, but the sound flew away in the wind so quickly that it was hardly heard.

'Good, you can neigh as much as you like out here,' Anna shouted.

It was terribly windy out there

Of course people could see the pony as the train went past, but Anna thought that that did not matter, as nobody would be able to catch up with the train.

'How surprised they will be,' Anna thought. 'Stay here for a moment, Danny, I'll come straight back.'

Anna walked cheerfully back through the carriages. She was not worried that anyone would go on to the platform at the end of the train. Danny would certainly be left in peace.

When she got back to their compartment she woke Nicholas and told him how well everything had worked out.

Nicholas thumped her on the back.

'Bravo!' he said. 'Why didn't we think of that before?'

'He couldn't have stayed there all night, he would have frozen to death,' Anna protested.

'Are you awake already?' asked Auntie suddenly. She sat up, put on her violet-coloured bed-jacket and looked down at them in a friendly way.

'Well, I never! It's half past five already. We must have slept for quite a few hours. Are you tired, children?'

'No, not a bit,' Anna replied. 'Good morning, Auntie!'

'We are as fit as fiddles,' Nicholas said.

He got up and stood in the middle of the floor so that he could have a good stretch.

Then the train started behaving rather strangely. The floor which had been shaking like a rattlesnake began to twitch. The drinking glasses and the water jug shook on their holders on the wall, and the coats jumped on their hooks. The train was going to stop. Nicholas and Anna gasped.

'Are we there already?' Nicholas shouted.

'Oh no, I suppose it must be Järna or possibly Södertälje,' Auntie replied.

Nicholas rushed out. Anna would have liked to go too as she realized that he was going to look after Danny and see that nobody took him. But she dared not leave Auntie.

'Did you sleep well, Auntie?'

'No, I had the most terrible dreams,' she replied. 'All about horses: horses stamping and horses laughing and horses biting the guard. The last dream I had twice, just to be on the safe side!'

'Were they nice horses?' Anna asked.

'No, they all looked just like the guard of this train,' Auntie replied.

She swung her legs over the edge of her bunk and carefully climbed down her little ladder.

'Perhaps we had better start getting dressed,' she said. 'I'll get ready first and then you can have a wash after me.'

Nicholas flung the door open and rushed in.

'Would you mind going out for a moment, Nicholas, so that I can get dressed?' Aunt Tina said to him kindly. 'It won't take long.'

Nicholas rushed out again.

Anna stared after him. He had grabbed Danny's bag, his own rucksack and a lot of other things.

What if Auntie caught sight of the pony's bag! But Nicholas was already gone. Anna wanted to go after him to find out what he was up to, but Auntie was in the way. Instead Anna pressed her nose against the window, as if that would make it possible for her to see the last carriage.

Auntie had a good wash. She had put all her bottles of scent and mouthwash and things on the shelf by the mirror, and was being as thorough as though she were in her own bathroom at home. Suddenly she turned round.

'Is somebody crying?' she asked. 'What is the matter, Anna? Aren't you happy to be going home?'

'Oh yes, it's nothing,' Anna murmured.

'But something *is* the matter, I can hear that,' Auntie said and came up to her. 'There now, dear, tell Auntie what it is so that she can comfort you!'

'I am looking at a poor little pony that they are just leading away on the station platform,' Anna whispered.

'Is that all?' Auntie exclaimed. 'What a thing to get upset about!'

'Of course it's something to get upset about,' Anna replied. 'He has been taken off the train. How will he ever manage in the world, Auntie? I shall never be happy again in my whole life if he is starved or badly treated!'

'Rubbish, Anna. He will be all right. His proper owner will collect him here and then they will live happily ever after, as they say in the story books,' Auntie said briskly.

'Do you really think so?' Anna sighed through her tears.

She saw some railwaymen leading Danny away towards the station, looking for somewhere to tie him up. They decided on a drainpipe by the corner of the main building. Anna bit her knuckles to stop herself from screaming. This was too terrible! They had found him! Why had Nicholas done nothing? She would have fought and kicked and screamed. Where *was* he, anyway?

Auntie patted Anna on the head.

'I wonder how long we are stopping at this station?' she said.

'We are off now, the floor is beginning to tickle. Can't you feel it, Auntie?' Anna had to cover her face with her hands. She could not bear to see Danny disappear.

'Oh yes, now we are moving,' Auntie said. 'Look at that boy who has gone out in his pyjamas! He must be even more interested in ponies than you are . . . funny how he resembles Nicholas . . . and he's got a rucksack too!'

'Ye-e-s,' Anna said breathlessly.

Nicholas had got off the train too; she could see him through her fingers.

'He was woken up too late, I suppose, and didn't have time to get dressed,' Auntie said. 'Well, well, well, the things people do! But ... no ... how ... but it's Nicholas! Nicholas!!' she shouted, 'Nicholas!!!'

'Good-bye, Nicholas, good-bye, pony!' Anna called and blew kisses to them both.

'I think I am going to faint!' Auntie exclaimed.

But she didn't, not a bit of it. She flung on her coat instead and rushed out into the corridor.

'What does the boy mean by getting off in green striped pyjamas?' she shouted. 'He must be walking in his sleep. Stop him! Let me past! I must get off!'

'Wait, Auntie! It's dangerous to get off, the trees are rushing past already. The train is going,' Anna shouted.

'Of course it's not! It couldn't go with Nicholas standing there on the platform. I forbid it to go! Don't touch me!'

'Please, please Auntie, *don't*!' Anna cried. 'Auntie, you mustn't, you are mad! Couldn't we pull the cord and stop the train instead?'

'That's an idea,' Auntie said.

She was suddenly calm again.

'Where is the cord? Is this it?'

'No, I don't think so, that must be the handle of the wash-basin,' Anna told her.

'But where, tell me! Somebody must have taken it!' Auntie looked round wildly, and there was the guard from yesterday, but she did not notice who she was talking to.

'I want to pull the communication cord and stop the train,' she said simply. 'Show me where it is.'

The guard raised his eyebrows. He was good at it, and they slid slowly up his forehead as though they were in a lift.

'Pull the cord?' he said. 'Why?'

'My little nephew got off at the wrong station. The boy in pyjamas. Why didn't you stop him?'

'As if I had nothing else to do!' the guard exclaimed. 'Besides, how should I know where people's nephews live? I couldn't know that he wasn't meant to get off there.'

'Don't talk, man, pull the cord and stop the train!'

That settled it. The guard rose to the occasion and to the importance of his duty. He planted himself, with arms crossed, in front of the cord and puffed himself out with a deep breath.

'We aren't going to pull no cord here!' he declared. 'It's there for serious accidents. You'll have to ring the station when we get to Stockholm, and tell them to put him on the next train. The boy won't come to any harm. He can sit in the waiting-room and read the time-tables like everybody else.'

And the train rattled on towards Stockholm.

Nicholas and Danny on their Own

Nicholas turned round and waved towards the train absent-mindedly. Off it went with Aunt Tina and Anna. He saw Aunt Tina – she looked surprised. Good to be rid of them, he thought. They would only make matters worse.

He walked round the corner of the station and put his rucksack down. What luck that he had managed to grab his clothes: everything except shoes. Never mind, he could wear his slippers. He started getting dressed.

Somebody came out of the waiting-room and seemed very amused at the sight of Nicholas.

'You must have got off at the last moment,' he said.

'Better late than never,' Nicholas replied.

He felt grown-up and independent. He had probably aged about ten years in the last few minutes. That would make him nineteen now, and that was the age he felt. People should not come along and make fun of him. He would rescue his Danny or die, only he had to get dressed first.

He put on his trousers on top of the pyjamas, as he did not want to stand there with nothing on. Then he put on his vest and pullover instead of the pyjama top.

He had also left his jacket on the train, but that could not be helped. Now he was ready for the rescue operation. He did up his rucksack and went back to Danny.

'Inspector, what shall we do with this pony that was on the express? There is no address label on him!' Nicholas heard someone shout.

'I'll cope with him in a minute, but come and help me get this stuff out of the way first,' the inspector replied.

Nicholas stepped forward.

'Could I help to hold the horse?' he asked.

The railwayman looked at him.

'You could put him over there on the other side of the road where he can graze by the ditch until we know what to do with him. Not by the kiosk, but a bit farther away so that he doesn't spoil the lawn. Some fool put him on the last platform of the express train,' he continued. 'People are crazy! Real vandals!'

'Perhaps they knew no better,' Nicholas suggested.

The inspector shouted again. He had a lot of goods to deal with, and needed help.

'I'll look after the pony for as long as you like,' Nicholas offered. 'I shan't leave him for a moment.'

'Good,' the man replied.

Nicholas went up to Danny. He stroked his muzzle and scratched his forehead and patted his flank on the right. Danny had cried in terror when he was lifted down on to the station platform and had bitten the hand of one of the railwaymen. He must have been very frightened. Nicholas felt rather guilty that he had not dared to help him then. He should have come forward and said: 'It's my horse. Don't touch him!' But then he would not have been able to rescue Danny now without anyone knowing that he was the owner.

Danny nudged his hand and sniffed in his pockets for rusks. But Nicholas had none. He untied the pony and started to walk round the corner of the station.

He walked as far as he dared along the edge of the ditch. Then he turned round to see if he was being watched. The inspector was standing with his hands on his hips, looking at him.

'Couldn't I put him in that field over there?'

The inspector had a look.

'Yes, put him there,' he shouted, 'but make sure you shut the gate.'

Nicholas walked on with Danny. He felt so happy that he thought it must show, even from the back. The field was some distance away and there was a bend in the road at that spot. If he started running there he

Then he turned round to see if he was being watched

would soon be out of sight. He walked very calmly and spoke to Danny in a low voice.

'You'll see, we shall fool them. Just take it gently!'

Danny neighed and nodded his head. You could tell he understood everything.

When he reached the field Nicholas looked back again. There was nobody to be seen by the station or at the windows. Just to be on the safe side he led Danny into the field through the gate and away among the trees. When they had waited for a while they got out through a place where the fence sagged, so that it was easy to jump over. Nicholas got up on Danny's back to start riding in earnest.

'Well, now let's ride to Stockholm,' he said.

Danny set off.

It was quite a while before they came to a bigger road.

'How can I tell if I am riding in the right direction?' Nicholas wondered. However, he soon came to a signpost with STOCKHOLM 45 KM. on it.

'That is quite a long way,' Nicholas said. 'Forty-five kilometres – can you walk that far in a day, Danny?'

Danny neighed. It sounded like 'Naay'.

'Can't you?' Nicholas asked. 'Surely you can walk ten kilometres in two hours, because I can. Forty-five, that would take, let me think ... nine hours. Then we would be there by three o'clock. No, that would be too much. Could you manage it in two days?'

'Nay-ay-ay,' Danny said again.

'But that is only four and a half hours a day. Well, perhaps you are right, it is a bit much. I can't sit here like this for very long. We'll have to do it in three days.'

'Nay-ay-ay,' Danny said.

'You are crazy, Danny. It really must not take more than three days. If Auntie has to sit waiting for us for three days at the central station she'll be so cross that she'll explode. You silly little pony!'

He patted Danny on the neck.

Then Danny was off again. He didn't seem to think they should waste time talking.

Nicholas held on. Riding was not easy. He had no saddle and no stirrups and only a halter to steer with, and he got tired very quickly.

Nicholas felt that he had been riding for hours when he reached a large farm. They had left the station behind and there was no danger of their being followed.

'Shall we go in here and ask if we can telephone home to let them know that we are on our way?' Nicholas said to Danny. 'I needn't tell them about you. I'll just speak to Mummy and say with a mysterious voice, "Don't be worried. Nicholas will be back in a few days." Then they will stop wondering what has happened.'

Danny nodded. He seemed to agree to most things. Nicholas patted him again.

The big farmyard was quite empty, but a large lorry stood by a stand for milk-churns. Ten huge churns had already been put on the lorry and five more were waiting to be loaded. The door of the dairy was open. Somebody must be in there.

Nicholas dismounted. He felt very stiff from the ride. He was tired of sitting and one of his feet had gone to sleep. When he tried to stand up straight, his knees seemed to stay bent. He listened to what was going on in the cow-shed. There was a lot of clanking and rattling in the dairy.

'Perhaps this is not an ordinary farm at all,' Nicholas thought. 'You can never know what kind of people live here. They may be gun-smugglers and safe-blowers and other dangerous types. Perhaps they are pretending to be farmers so that no one will suspect them.'

There was more rattling from the shed. Were they loading revolvers and guns? Nicholas dared not go in.

'Don't wake the neighbours,' he heard a voice say.

'If they haven't woken up other mornings, why should they wake today?' a woman's voice replied.

Could there be lady gun-smugglers too? Nicholas wondered.

'Don't be too sure. It is best to be careful,' the first voice said.

That sounded mysterious!

'Hurry up, so I can go. I don't want to go tearing along the roads so fast that I get the police after me,' the man's voice said.

Nicholas decided to go and hide with Danny, but at that moment a woman came out with a large milk-churn on a trolley.

'Goodness, what a fright you gave me!' she exclaimed when she saw Nicholas. 'I thought you were a robber, or something, standing there! Who are you, anyway?'

'My name is Nicholas, and I'm riding home to Stockholm on this pony. But I am awfully tired.'

'That is nothing to what he must be,' the man said who had come out too. He pointed to Danny and then walked over to pat him. Danny sniffed at him contentedly.

'Whoever gave you the idea of riding all the way? Very silly, I think it is,' the woman said.

'It is my idea,' said Nicholas. 'I was going to surprise Mummy and Daddy. They don't know that I am riding home.'

The man laughed.

'I don't think you will manage it,' he said. 'The pony will get a bad back, and you will have blisters all over before you are half-way. If I don't give you a lift in the milk lorry, that is.'

'Of course you ought to go with Henry instead,' the woman went on. 'Now don't be silly! It is bad for a little pony like this to walk so far with you on its back.'

'Yes, that's just what I think,' the man said. 'Why do you have to insist on riding? They'll only be angry with you at home.'

Nicholas was struck dumb. He didn't insist on riding at all if he and Danny could get a lift, but he hadn't had a chance to say so.

'Now you do as I tell you,' the woman went on. 'You'll thank me for it when you get home, and your Mummy and Daddy will too, I should think.'

'No doubt about that,' Henry added.

'Thank you very much, we would certainly like a lift,' Nicholas managed to say at last.

'That's settled then. I knew you would come to your senses and do the right thing,' the woman said. 'You can go all the way to the dairy depot in Stockholm.'

'Will we pass Mälarhöjden? That's where I live,' Nicholas said.

'We can do. It depends on which route I take. Still, I don't mind if I go out of my way a bit!'

The Reunion

Auntie got off the train with her newly packed trunk and left five empty boxes in the compartment. She walked past the guard without giving him so much as a glance, and then she called a porter. She held Anna tightly by the hand, and dared not let go of her for a moment.

'Well, here we are,' she said, 'and everyone can relax. But *we* can't. We must get the next train back to look for Nicholas.'

'Poor Auntie, you must be so tired. Couldn't I go back on my own to look for Nicholas?' Anna suggested.

'That would just be a fine thing, wouldn't it! Then I would have lost you too. And I'd get back home to Mummy and Daddy empty-handed,' Auntie moaned. 'What shall I do if something happens to Nicholas?'

'That isn't very likely. He keeps saying that nothing ever happens to him. He would be very pleased if he had a gorilla and some cannibals after him,' Anna said reassuringly.

Auntie had her trunk put in the left-luggage office and then she found a telephone to ring the station where Nicholas had got off. Evidently the inspector answered the phone.

'Hallo? Hallo, is that the inspector?' Auntie said. 'My name is Miss Nilson and I want some information about our Nicholas who was left behind at your station. He got off the train without anyone knowing and somebody must look after him ... what's that? Describe him? Well, he has brown eyes, I think. Yes, that's right.'

'Blue,' said Anna.

'And he is rather small . . . yes, that's right. If he has a mark on his forehead? No, I don't think so. Has Nicholas a birthmark on his forehead, Anna?'

'No, but there's one on his back,' Anna replied.

'He has a mark on his back,' Auntie went on. 'Yes, we are sure.'

Auntie sounded quite hopeful.

'And white socks? Yes, why? On all four legs ... what do you mean by four? Surely you mean both,' Auntie said impatiently. 'Has he four white legs and a long tail? Really, now everybody must have gone mad! Have you ever seen a little boy with four legs? Yes, a *boy*! What did you think we were talking about?'

'Let me explain,' Anna cried.

But it was too late. The man at the other end had slammed the receiver down angrily.

Auntie went to pieces completely. She leaned against the telephone and began to cry. Anna hugged her and patted her but she just went on sobbing. She brought a handkerchief out of her blue bag to wipe her eyes, but as soon as she did, new tears welled up.

'Dear little Anna, I don't know if you realize how serious this is,' Auntie sighed. 'Mummy and Daddy allowed me to take you to Copenhagen, and they trusted me, and now I shall have to ring up and tell them that I have lost Nicholas. I can't tell you how desperate I feel. I shall have to inform the police and have a message broadcast on the radio as I did when you got lost in Copenhagen.'

'Did it help?' Anna asked.

'No, it didn't, because you turned up anyhow, but it would have done. We must leave no stone unturned. But first of all we must tell Mummy and Daddy everything.'

This made Anna almost as upset as Auntie. To tell everything now was the worst thing they could possibly do. Daddy and Mummy would be worried about Nicholas getting lost and they would be cross when he was found and if they knew that it was all because of a miniature pony . . .

'Oh Auntie, they'll be so cross,' she exclaimed. 'Don't tell them anything. I remember what happened when I lost my green gloves. Mummy carried on for several days. Just imagine what she will be like now we have lost the whole of Nicholas! Couldn't we try ringing the station again? They would probably know better, now they have had time to think. We'll explain at once that it is a boy we are looking for.'

Auntie sighed and blew her nose.

'No, we'll have to get the first train back, as I said. We must go and find out when it leaves.'

They went together to the inquiries desk. The next train, they said, would be in one hour and fifty-five minutes. Auntie wrung her hands in despair, but Anna comforted her again.

'That isn't even two hours,' she said. 'Daddy is at the office and nobody is coming to meet us, so nobody will notice if we go back to that station. And we can always ring them from there when we have found Nicholas. Once we've got him, it won't matter if we are a little late.'

Auntie was inclined to agree with Anna. They went to the refreshment counter and ordered tea and strong coffee and sandwiches. It was a long time before their order came, but when it did, Auntie finished her coffee in one gulp.

'I wish I had a pill to calm me down,' she said.

Anna patted Auntie's hand and put two lumps of sugar in her coffee.

'Have some more coffee instead, Auntie; that will make you feel better.' They went on sitting there for a long time.

From where Anna was sitting she could see a nice little train in a glass case on the main hall of the station. But she dared not point it out to Auntie – probably Auntie did not want to think about trains more than she had to. It was very attractive though. A father with three little daughters stood looking at the engine.

'Lift me up, Daddy!' one of them said.

'I want to see too,' the second said.

'So do I,' the third one went on. 'What do they have these baby engines for? And why is it in a glass box like a goldfish? Is it an under-water engine?'

'No, it is a model of a real engine. If you put money in that slot the train will go,' the man told them.

But he should never have done that.

'Please, Daddy, put the money in, just once. We want to see the wheels go round,' the little girls cried.

'Well, just once, then,' the father replied.

He looked through all his pockets and found a coin hiding away somewhere.

The smallest girl put the coin in the slot, and the wheels of the train started to go round. The pistons moved and there was a humming noise.

'Is that the end already?' the girls asked as soon as it stopped.

'Couldn't we take the lid off and let the train run on the floor to see how fast it goes?' the eldest girl asked.

'No, we must go home now,' the man answered.

'Just *once* more,' the little girl begged.

'Just once!' the third one said.

The father sighed unconvincingly. He was obviously prepared to go through the whole performance again. He found another coin.

'Now it is my turn to put it in,' the middle girl said.

Anna sighed. She knew exactly what would happen next. Auntie sat there worrying and looking utterly dejected. It was such a pity that she couldn't think of something amusing for a little while, and enjoy herself. The train started going again and then stopped.

'It was much quicker this time,' the middle girl said. 'Just once more. The very last go.'

'Yes, just once more, the very last go,' the eldest girl said.

And then the little one chirped:

'Yes, just once more. The very last go!'

'All right then, but this is the last time. Then we *must* go home,' the father replied.

'Just as I thought,' Anna said to herself.

The man looked through his pockets again, but this time he really didn't seem to have another coin for the machine.

'They'll go on looking until it is time for our train,' Anna thought crossly.

'She can put mine in for me. I was going to do it anyway,' a boy said who was standing next to the father. He must have been tired of waiting too. Anna sighed again.

At that moment Auntie got up with a muffled scream.

'Nicholas!' she shouted, so that the boy and the father and children all turned round.

Then Anna saw that the boy was her own brother! Auntie and Anna rushed down into the big hall. By some miracle Auntie remembered to grab her bag.

'How did you get here?' she cried.

They both gave him a big hug.

'I have been looking for you for a long time,' Nicholas said, 'But I couldn't find you. I thought you hadn't got here.'

'Tell us what happened,' Auntie said.

'Oh, nothing much. I got a lift in a car, and they took me all the way home. Then I came by underground to look for you. I just went into the garage first and left something there.'

'Your luggage,' Auntie nodded. 'How sensible. Didn't you go up and say hallo to Mummy?'

'No, I didn't have time. Anyway, I thought it would be better if we all got home together.'

Auntie hugged him again.

'Oh, it's too good to be true!' she murmured. 'I am the world's happiest aunt. We thought we would never see you again!'

They hurried off to the left-luggage office to fetch Auntie's trunk and Anna's suitcase, and then they went to the line of taxis waiting outside the station. Auntie was in such a hurry now that it was difficult to keep up with her. In no time at all they were sitting in the taxi bumping along on Stockholm's familiar old cobblestones and cracked asphalt, out towards their suburb.

'I forgot to take off my shoes to see what it is like to walk on Swedish soil again,' Nicholas said.

Auntie was speechless with joy. She sat with an arm round each of them, staring straight ahead with a smile on her lips. Every now and then she sighed.

'Are you going to tell Mummy and Daddy about ... Nicholas?' Anna asked as they got nearer home.

Auntie woke up from her thoughts with a start, looking rather guilty.

'I don't know,' she replied. 'I was wondering about that myself.'

'Perhaps it would be a pity to worry them, sort of ... straight away,' Nicholas suggested.

'You mean, we should spare their nerves?' Auntie asked.

'Well, as we found each other again, it's not worth mentioning, is it?'

'No, perhaps you are right. We'll say nothing to start with, and then maybe, later on ... leave it to me.'

'Oh yes, we'll leave it to you, Aunt Tina!' Nicholas and Anna said together and smiled at each other.

All is Well

Lunch was ready when they got home. Mummy had cooked a mushroom omelette for Aunt Tina and sausages and chips for Nicholas and Anna, and there was a vase of blue flowers by Auntie's place.

'How lovely to have you home again, safe and sound!' were Mummy's first words. 'I have been waiting and waiting. I thought you would arrive earlier – the train must have been delayed. But never mind, the main thing is that you are here. Do tell me how it has been!'

'Wonderful, splendid, terrific fun,' Anna said. 'So exciting that we almost died!'

'No, she's exaggerating,' Nicholas said. 'It was just super. The best time I've had in my life!'

'Yes, very pleasant indeed,' Auntie agreed.

Mother looked at her searchingly. She seemed to understand what Auntie was feeling.

'Now have a good lunch,' she said, 'and then you can lie down and have a rest. I want you to tell me all about it, but there's no hurry.'

'I'm not too tired to talk,' Auntie said. 'Of course we had our little ups and downs, nothing to worry about, but still, I won't deny that I am pleased to be back. But I must say that Nicholas and Anna have been most kind and helpful all the time. They have been considerate and well-behaved and comforted me and helped me as well as they could when things got difficult.'

'Yes, we really did,' Nicholas and Anna agreed.

Mother nodded and gave Aunt Tina some salad.

'I am sure you deserve a medal, Tina,' she said. 'You must tell us the details when we are all assembled.'

'Is Daddy coming home to lunch, then?' Nicholas asked.

Mummy nodded and looked out of the window.

'Yes, he said he wanted to check you all in as soon as possible, and make quite sure that Aunt Tina had survived. I think I can hear the car now.'

Nicholas flew up from his chair so quickly that it almost fell backwards. He looked like Tarzan, son of the apes, when stampeding elephants are approaching.

'Is he here already?' he exclaimed. 'I hope he doesn't drive so fast that he collides with things in the garage . . . He *will* look where he is going, I hope.'

Anna had also jumped up.

'Ooooh, yes! He mustn't drive into the garage without putting the lights on. If he does, I'll go mad!'

'What on earth is the matter with you two?' Mother asked.

'Nothing,' they replied.

At that moment Daddy came in. He looked round and said hallo to them all. He held out his hand to Aunt Tina, and smiled all over his face.

'So you've all survived,' he said. 'Tell me everything about it!'

He looked as if he had never seen a pony in his life. Nicholas and Anna could not take their eyes off him. He sat down quite calmly and helped himself to all the chips that were left.

'Oh, there's nothing to tell,' Aunt Tina said modestly. 'We just went there, and then we came back again.'

'No, really! You can't get us to believe that! We won't let you off so lightly. We've read your postcards over and over, so we do know a little already.'

Auntie collected herself and looked at Nicholas and Anna.

'Well, I hardly remember what I have written,' she said. 'I may have mentioned something about losing Anna at the Zoo that day when they wanted to see if they had won anything in the pony-lottery. I don't understand how we became separated. It is a complete mystery to me, but she found her way back to the hotel, all by herself.'

'Did she really!' Mummy exclaimed.

'Yes, and then there was a spot of trouble at the hotel. The hall porter said that the children were stamping on the floor and playing horses in their room. But it was one of the maids banging about with a vacuum-cleaner, I heard it myself, and Anna did too,' Auntie continued.

'Really!' Mother said.

'There is nothing worse than staying in hotels with kids. I did warn you,' Daddy said.

Aunt Tina shook her head bravely.

'They couldn't help that,' she said. 'But the most ridiculous thing was that stupid hotel porter who took it into his head to neigh in the children's wardrobe. What a thing to get up to, just as we were about to leave too! But do you think he would admit that he had ever set foot in the cupboard, oh no . . .'

'A neighing porter in the wardrobe,' Mummy said thoughtfully. 'It does sound a bit strange . . .'

'I still don't know what he was doing in there,' Auntie continued. 'Well, then Anna and Nicholas chose to empty all the clothes out of my big trunk before they sent it off to the station. "The man didn't say that he was to take the clothes too," those little sillies said. Well, that didn't matter at all. I just took it as a joke.'

'What ridiculous nonsense!' Daddy exclaimed. 'Really, children, how could you be so stupid?'

He managed to look quite cross for a moment before Auntie continued, but Mummy said nothing at all. She was looking at Nicholas and Anna very closely.

'Then we had some trouble with a mad guard on the train who kept waking us up to tell us all the passengers' horrible dreams.' Auntie went on.

'What did they dream about? Was it horses, by any chance?' Mummy asked.

'Yes, can you imagine! How did you guess? In the end I thought I heard horses myself,' Auntie said. 'And the children pottered around half the night, having drinks and things to eat and scratching each other behind the ears . . .'

'Surely you could have been quiet and behaved yourselves properly as I told you to,' Daddy said.

Nicholas and Anna were afraid to answer. They did not want to get Daddy into a bad mood. Mummy was beginning to look strange too.

'Oh, let's forget it!' Auntie exclaimed. 'I expect they found it difficult to sleep after everything we had seen and heard. Well, now there isn't much more to tell. Anna was very upset when she saw a pony taken off the train at a station, and I had to comfort her and then . . .'

Auntie hesitated.

'And then, that is all,' she said.

'I wonder,' Mummy said thoughtfully. 'I am beginning to think there is something behind all this. I am beginning to believe – '

Auntie, Nicholas and Anna all protested.

'No, no, no,' Auntie said. 'Everything went so well!'

'It's nothing, Mummy, nothing at all!' Nicholas and Anna both shouted.

Daddy looked very cheerful.

'Things could have been worse. I have hardly been able to work, I have been thinking about you so much this week. I imagined the most terrible things happening. But here you are, safe and sound. We must celebrate!'

He lifted Anna up in the air and punched Nicholas playfully, and smiled at Aunt Tina.

'You are better at coping than I thought you would be. And here at home nothing has happened either, except that I was nearly late for lunch because I came across a pony in the garage. He was standing quite peacefully in there, drinking water out of the bucket I use for cleaning the car.'

'Oh, did you, Daddy? Was he sweet?' Anna shouted.

'Did you like him?' Nicholas asked.

'No, really, now I understand everything!' Mummy exclaimed.

Nicholas and Anna began to jump with excitement. Nicholas shook Daddy to stop him from thinking, and Anna tried to put her hand over Mummy's mouth.

'Don't say anything, Mummy, please don't say anything!'

'Did you like him, Daddy?' Nicholas asked seriously.

'Yes, it was certainly the prettiest pony I have ever

seen,' Daddy replied. 'But I can't understand who could have put him in there. Perhaps somebody from the riding-school made a mistake. Pity it's not ours, so that you could have a ride.'

Mummy put her hands to her face.

'Now you've said the wrong thing!' she cried. 'You'll regret that.'

But she couldn't help laughing all the same. Daddy didn't seem to understand at all. He looked at Mummy, and at Nicholas and Anna who were dancing round him wildly. They shouted and whooped so that the house seemed to shake.

'Would you let us ride the pony if it were ours? Say yes, Daddy, say yes!' they shouted.

'I advise you to say no,' Mummy said to him.

But Daddy still did not understand.

'Why not?' he asked. 'Of course I would let them. *If* the pony were theirs, that is. But of course he isn't.'

'Yes, yes, that's just what he is,' Anna declared with an impressive voice. 'He's our own Danny, and you said that we could keep him!'

'You have promised!' Nicholas shouted.

Daddy resigned himself to fate and decided to accept it bravely.

'What pony is that you are talking about?' Auntie asked. 'Where did you get him from? You must tell me all about it!'

PONIES PLOT

C. Northcote Parkinson

The world is full of books about ponies, written for children. This is completely different, a book about children, written for ponies. Instead of the child teaching the pony how to jump – as if it didn't *know* – it is the pony who teaches the child how to ride.

From a pony's point of view, all riding schools have the same thing wrong with them: they are for children who can't ride. As soon as a child becomes bearable, she vanishes and has a pony of her own, and her place is taken by another. The newcomers are certain to scream when the pony walks and as likely to fall off as soon as it comes to a halt. 'Here we go again,' the ponies grumble, and who can blame them?

HORSE IN THE HOUSE

William Corbin

Melanie Webb was one of those girls who can't live without a horse, and the one she had was a winner, a white palomino stallion called Orbit. He was never out of her thoughts, and he waited all day for the moment she came home from school to ride him.

Then Mom and Pop went off to San Francisco, giving Melanie a chance to put her cherished plan into action – her secret wish to bring Orbit inside the house. One night Melanie went out to the barn to say goodnight to Orbit, but he was gone and the unoccupied stable was intolerably desolate and empty. Melanie felt useless, like a captain without a ship. Yet somewhere Orbit existed, and somewhere she was sure, locked in her head was some little memory, a shred of a clue to the thief.

BREAK FOR FREEDOM

Ewan Clarkson

Syla was a mink, and so dark brown she looked almost black.

The cage where she lived was identical with all the others, except for one thing – there was a loose staple in the floor of her sleeping box. And that was the way that Syla escaped from the fur farm to find a new life, free in a remote valley on the edge of Dartmoor, free to hunt and fish and play, and also to face the dangers of traps or sudden chills or fierce animals.

Ewan Clarkson is an expert naturalist and makes a fascinating story of Syla's year on the moor, her brief courtship with another escaped mink and her life with her cubs. At the same time he tells us about all the other inhabitants of Dartmoor, the birds and insects, snakes and rodents, till the moor seems as busy and complicated as the greatest human city.

For readers of eleven upwards.

THE CUSTER WOLF

Roger Caras

One April five wolf cubs were born in a cave under a tree stump. One was white, and men would come to call him by a name that would live in history, for this was the beginning of the legend of the Custer Wolf.

This wolf inexplicably grew up different from any other. He was a beautiful but solitary animal and as he grew it became clear that he killed for the love of killing and terrorized a huge area round the town of Custer for six whole years.

Sometimes he killed thirty cattle in a week, more than he could possibly eat, and he took incredible chances, yet he escaped every trap that was set and every gun that was fired. Small wonder that the men believed the white wolf was charmed.

COME HOME, BRUMBY

Mary Elwyn Patchett

15-year-old Joey had for years dreamed of fencing in the brumby herd and breeding to improve the stock, so when Florian, the beautiful white stallion he had tamed, escaped to follow Brumby the wild stallion and his herd on their seasonal migration, Joey decided to follow the herd himself and drive them home single-handed.

For readers of nine and over.

LEON

Helen Griffiths

The puppy howled and felt the hot gushing of his own blood and began to whimper again, no longer even trying to escape. With one more blow the crow would destroy him. . . . But that blow never comes. Instead he feels the gentle hands of Hilario, the farm boy who dreams of being a doctor.

But as Leon grows into a magnificent creature of strength and courage, his life and fortunes change. His young master is forced to sell him to Don Augustín, the local land owner, but the rich man cannot buy his loyalty or love and the pair are briefly reunited.

Then comes the horror of the Spanish Civil War and Leon is left starving and bewildered. His new master savagely ill-treats him and he becomes an outlaw, killing the sheep it was once his pride to protect.

A vivid and moving story for readers of 10 to 13.